BLOOM
Founded by | arihant

Olympiad ACE

A Comprehensive Practice Book

for School Olympiads & Talent Search Exams

SCIENCE

Class 8

by
Bhawna Joshi

Olympiad ACE

BLOOM

Bloom Cap Edu Ventures Pvt. Ltd.

Administrative & Production Office

'Ramchhaya' 4577/15, Agarwal Road, Darya Ganj, New Delhi -110002
Tele: 011- 47630600, 43518550

PRICE: ₹125.00

Published by Arihant Publications (I) Ltd.

For further information about the books log on to
www.bloomcap.org

Follow us on

Preface

"Future belongs to those Who prepares for it today"

School Olympiads are National & International level competitions conducted by different Government, Non-Government & Educational Organisations with the purpose of making the children ready to face competitive exams.

The challenging Questions asked in Olympiads motivate them to learn more & more and bring out the best result with improved academic performance. The Awards & Scholarship offered by Olympiads motivate children to aspire & strive for doing better and emerge out to be the best.

Science Olympiads

Being a Scientist or Engineer or Doctor has always been a dream of each school going child. A good command over Science is a must for any of these. Questions of Science Olympiads are structured to help students to develop scientific temperament & motivate them to understand the concepts of science. They also focuses on improving existing knowledge of a student by adding more information.

'Bloom Science Olympiad Study Book Class 8' is a perfect resource to Study & Practice for Olympiad Exams and other National & State Level Talent Search Exams & Other Competitions.

Some Special Features of Bloom Science Olympiad Study Books are;

- Chapterwise Exercises having different types of Objective Questions; Analytical, Applications, Remembering etc, at par with the Olympiad Level.
- Detailed Explanation for each question.
- Olympiad Pattern Practice Sets at the end.

This book is prepared by Expert Panel with the utmost care, still if you have any suggestions regarding its improvement then feel free to contact us at support@bloomcap.org. We will try to inculcate your suggestions in the further editions.

Contents

01. Crop Production and Management 1-6
02. Microorganisms : Friend & Foe 7-13
03. Coal and Petroleum 14-20
04. Combustion and Flame 21-27
05. Conservation of Plants and Animals 28-30
06. Reproduction in Animals 31-33
07. Reaching the Age of Adolescence 34-36
08. Force and Pressure 37-44
09. Friction 45-49
10. Sound 50-56
11. Chemical Effects of Electric Current 57-63
12. Some Natural Phenomenon 64-67
13. Light 68-72
- Practice Set 1 73-81
- Practice Set 2 82-89
- Hints & Solutions 90-108

Chapter 01

Crop Production and Management

1 Mark Questions

1. Which of the following is not a cereal crop?
(a) Maize (b) Ragi
(c) Bean (d) Barley

2. Some Rabi and Kharif crops are listed below in the box.

Maize, Paddy, Groundnut, Cotton, Mustard, Pea, Wheat, Gram

How many of the following can be considered as Kharif's crop ?
(a) 4 (b) 3 (c) 5 (d) 6

3. Ram, a farmer is in the process of selecting good quality seeds. He puts a handful of seeds in water. After sometime, he noticed '*X*' seeds settled at the bottom while '*Y*' seeds floated on the top.
Which seeds he should not select and Why?
(a) *X* seeds, they are heavy
(b) *Y* seeds, they are damaged and hollow
(c) *X* seeds, they are not healthy
(d) Both seeds, they are unhealthy

4. Farmers often add chemical fertilisers in soil to increase their crop output. However, this practice increase the .... level in soil.
Fill the blank by selecting a correct option.
(a) acid (b) alkaline (c) salt (d) neutral

5. '*X*' is a certain type of substance made from inorganic salts especially for plants when they are deficient for a certain nutrient. '*Y*' is a common type of substance for crops obtained by decomposing dead plants and animal wastes. What is '*X*' and '*Y*'?
(a) Comport, Weedicide
(b) Fertiliser, Organic manure
(c) Ferticide, Inorganic salts
(d) Manure, Vermicompost.

6. Which of the following is not true for fertilisers?
(a) They increase the yield
(b) Their excessive use disturbs the balance of nutrients in soil
(c) They are generally used in small quantity
(d) They are environment friendly

7. In a town, where water scarcity is a major issue, farmers will be advised to use which method for watering their crops?

(a) Sprinkler (b) Drip system
(c) Moat (d) Dhekli

8. ……… tool is used with a tractor for sowing seeds in a field. Filling the blank by selecting a correct option.

(a) Thresher (b) Hoe
(c) Seed Drill (d) Plough

9. Complete the analogy shown below
Seed drill : Sowing : ..... : Removing weeds

(a) Plough (b) Cultivator
(c) Hoe (d) None of these

10. Ploughing helps in ……… of roots of growing plants. Fill in the blank by selecting a correct option.

(a) penetration
(b) transplantation
(c) sowing
(d) protection

11. Before sowing the seeds in a field, the soil is broken down to the size of grain for a better yield of crops. Which of the following pairs of tools can be associated with these processes?

(a) Plough, hoe and cultivator
(b) Tractor, hoe and seed drill
(c) Plough, seed drill and tractor
(d) Bullock, tiller and tractor

12. The use of machinery in agriculture helps to

I. increase the crop yield.
II. get the job done faster.
III. reduce the dependency on human and animal labour.

Choose the correct option.

(a) Both I and II (b) Both I and III
(c) Both II and III (d) I, II and III

13. Microorganisms are known to cause various diseases in crop plants affecting the overall yield.
Identify the organisms which cause disease 'blight of potato'.

(a) Fungus (b) Virus
(c) Protozoan (d) Bacteria

14. Rice and soyabean are crops grown during the onset of monsoon season because

(a) they require more water for growth
(b) they require more sunlight
(c) they require less temperature
(d) All of the above

15. In three agricultural fields *P*, *Q* and *R*, crops are planted in patterns as shown below.

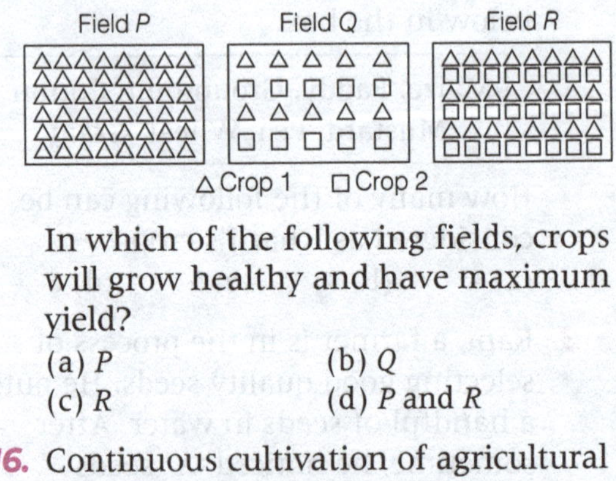

In which of the following fields, crops will grow healthy and have maximum yield?

(a) *P* (b) *Q*
(c) *R* (d) *P* and *R*

16. Continuous cultivation of agricultural field results in depletion of soil nutrients. Given below are some methods to restore the fertility of soil

I. Land is left uncultivated for one or more season.
II. Addition of manure to soil.
III. Excessive use of fertilisers in agricultural field.
IV. Growing different crops alternately.

Select the correct method to restore soil fertility.

Codes

(a) I and II
(b) I, II and IV
(c) III and IV
(d) All of these

17. Read the statements given below.

I. Fertilizers are the chemical substances rich in particular nutrient.
II. Plants of same kind grown in a field on large scale is called crop.
III. Process of loosening and turning the soil is termed as threshing.
IV. Rearing of fishes for its various products is known as pisciculture.

Select the correct option, which is correct for above statements.

(a) I, II are correct
(b) I, II and IV are correct
(c) Only II is correct
(d) Only I is correct

18. Read the statements given below.

I. Fertilisers are used to increase the soil fertility.
II. Urea, ammonium sulphate and superphosphate are some fertilisers.

Select the option, which is correct for above statements?

(a) Both I and II are correct
(b) Only I is correct
(c) Both I and II are incorrect
(d) Only II is correct

19. Some insects or animals are listed below in the box.

Ladybug, Locusts, Praying mantis, Ground beetle, Frog, Earthworms, Wild boar.

How many of the following can be considered as farmer's friend?

(a) 3 (b) 5 (c) 4 (d) 6

20. A farmer has three crop fields and in all his fields weeds are growing. He sprayed weedicide in all the three. Given below is the time period when he sprayed weedicide.

Crop field	Time period of weedicide spray
I.	After flowering
II.	After full growth of weeds
III.	Before flowering and seed formation

Choose the correct crop field where the weedicide spray was effective.

(a) Both I and II (b) Only III
(c) Only I (d) Only II

21. Identify the statement which is incorrect w.r.t the figure shown below.

(a) It is a modern method of irrigation called the sprinkler system
(b) The water available in wells, canals and lakes is lifted up using this method
(c) Its cheaper but less efficient
(d) Human labour is used in this methods

22. Prerana went to her village during holidays. While on her way to a crop field, he saw a person with covered mouth spraying something on crops. She got worried about the crops and asked the person to stop. The person who was her neighbour smiled and explained her the purpose of his act. Prerana was happy to learn a new fact about learning. According to you what was the person doing?

(a) The person was spraying special chemicals called weedicides on his crops to kill unwanted plants in his field
(b) The person was spraying water on his crops to keep his crops hydrated
(c) The person was spraying fertilizers on his crops to provide nutrients in his field
(d) None of the above

23. Mayank went to his field and saw weeds growing there. Given below are the statements about the harmful effects of weeds on crop plants.

I. They interfere in harvesting.
II. They help crop plants to grow healthily.
III. They compete with crop plants for water nutrients, space and light.
IV. They affect the plant growth.

Choose the correct combination of statements
(a) I, III and IV
(b) Only III
(c) III and IV
(d) I, II, III and IV

24. Study the flowchart given below.

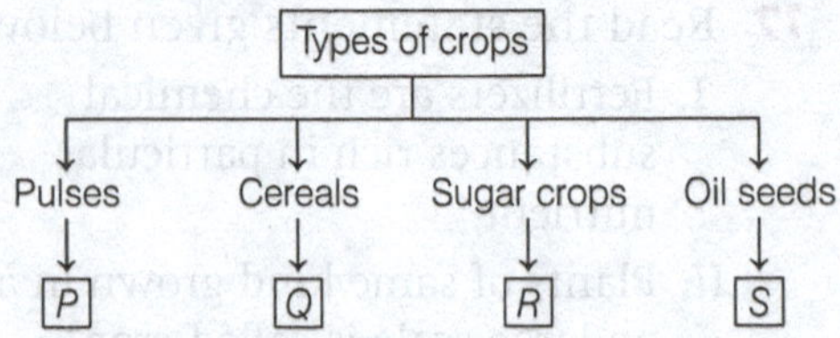

Select the correct statements w.r.t labelled parts.
(a) *P* could be ragi, while *R* could be beetroots
(b) *Q* could be beans, while *S* could be barley
(c) *P* could be legumes like gram or pea, while *S* could be mustard or groundnut
(d) *Q* could be potato or tapioca, while *R* could be sugarcane or beetroot

25. Terms related to agricultural practices are given below. Rearrange them in the correct sequence.
(a) Ploughing → Manuring → Sowing → Irrigation → Weeding → Harvesting
(b) Ploughing → Sowing → Manuring → Irrigation → Weeding → Harvesting
(c) Ploughing → Manuring → Irrigation → Sowing → Weeding → Harvesting
(d) Ploughing → Sowing → Manuring → Weeding → Irrigation → Harvesting

2 Marks Questions

26. Match the Column I and Column II and select the correct option from the codes given below

Column I	Column II
A. Thresher	1. Levelling of ploughed soil so as to prevent soil erosion
B. Hoe	2. For tilling the soil
C. Combine	3. Harvesting as well as threshing
D. Leveller	4. Threshing (separation of grains from chaff)

Codes

	A	B	C	D
(a)	4	2	3	1
(b)	1	2	3	4
(c)	4	3	2	1
(d)	1	4	2	3

27. Match the Column I with Column II and select the correct option from codes given below.

Column I	Column II
A. Threshing	1. Seed drill
B. *Rhizobium*	2. Separation of grain from the rest of the plant
C. Jute	3. Nitrogen fixation
D. Rubber	4. Plantation crop
E. Broadcasting of seeds	5. Fibre crop

Codes

	A	B	C	D	E
(a)	1	2	3	5	4
(b)	3	4	1	2	5
(c)	2	3	5	4	1
(d)	5	1	2	3	1

28. State (T) for True and (F) for False.

I. Using good quality seeds to the only criterion to get high yield.

II. Growing different crops in different seasons in the same field will deplete the soils of nutrients.

III. All crop plants are sown as seeds in the field.

IV. Cells of root nodules of leguminous plants fix nitrogen.

Codes

	I	II	III	IV		I	II	III	IV
(a)	F	T	T	F	(b)	F	F	F	F
(c)	F	F	F	T	(d)	T	F	F	F

29. Match the following columns.

Column I	Column II
A. Winnowing	1. Cotton
B. Weeding	2. 2, 4-D
C. Rabi season crop	3. Separating grains from harvested crop
D. Kharif season crop	4. Insect
E. Threshing	5. Pea
F. Honey	6. Separating grains from chaff

Codes

	A	B	C	D	E	F
(a)	6	2	5	1	3	4
(b)	1	2	3	4	5	6
(c)	6	5	4	3	2	1
(d)	6	2	5	1	4	3

30. Sprinklers help in water conservation alongwith an efficient system of irrigation for agricultural fields.

Identify the statements which supports the above claim.

I. Sprinklers use the low pressure of water flow to irrigate the field similar to rain fall.

II. They can cover a large circular area while irrigating the fields.

III. Water drops falls directly near the roots.

IV. It prevents water logging conditions in field.

Codes

(a) I and II (b) II and IV
(c) I, III and IV (d) All of these

31. Refer to the figures *X* and *Y* which represent specific agricultural processes shown below.

Select the correct statement w.r.t processes shown in figures *X* and *Y*.

I. *X* helps in removing weeds from crop plants, while *Y* is the addition of manures to the collected crops.

II. *X* separates harvested grains from their stalks and *Y* separate grains from the chaff.

III. *X* is tilling, while *Y* is manual sowing of seeds.

Which of the following options are correct for the figure?

(a) I is correct, but II and III are incorrect
(b) I and II are correct, but III is incorrect
(c) I is incorrect, but II and III are correct
(d) I and III are incorrect, but II is correct

32. Certain crops like beans, grams and peas are grown in soil where nitrogen levels need to be replenished. The main reason for adopting this practice is

I. They have *Rhizobium*, a bacteria living symbiotically within their roots.

II. These are leguminous plants.

III. They can directly absorb the atmospheric nitrogen for replenshing depleted nitrogen levels.

IV. These are non-green plants which can trap insects to absorb nitrogen.

Select the correct option.

(a) I and II
(b) I, III and IV
(c) III and IV
(d) I, II and III

33. Match the terms given in Column I with those of Column II. Select the correct option from the codes given below.

Column I	Column II
A. Silos	1. Fertilizer
B. Combines	2. Storage of grains
C. Urea	3. Sprinklers
D. Irrigation	4. Harvesting and threshing

Codes

	A	B	C	D
(a)	2	4	1	3
(b)	1	2	3	4
(c)	4	3	2	1
(d)	1	3	2	4

Chapter 02

Microorganisms : Friend & Foe

1 Mark Questions

1. Given below is a list of microorganisms based on their characteristic features. Pick the odd one out.

(a) *Amoeba* (b) *Paramecium*
(c) *Rhizobium* (d) *Plasmodium*

2. Read the following statements about protozoa.

I. They are visible only under a microscope.
II. They are mostly found in fresh water and in slimy moist soil.
III. *Penicillium* and *Spirogyra* are the examples of Protozoa.
IV. They have not the ability to move and find their food.

Which of the above statements is/are correct ?

(a) I and II (b) Only I
(c) I, II and IV (d) III and IV

3. Given below is a list of communicable diseases based on their causative agents. Pick the odd one out.

(a) Influenza (b) Chickenpox
(c) Typhoid (d) Common cold

4. Which list of characteristics describe a bacterium?

	Outer layer	Cytoplasm	Nuclear material
(a)	Cell wall	Present	Circular DNA
(b)	Cell wall	Present	One or many nuclei
(c)	No cell wall	Absent	Many chromosomes
(d)	Protein coat	Absent	DNA combined with protein

5. Which of the two microorganisms live in symbiotic association in lichens?

A. Fungus B. Protozoa
C. Bacteria D. Algae

Choose the correct option.

(a) A and B (b) B and C
(c) C and D (d) A and D

6. Observe the figures given below and identify the option which correctly pairs the organism which is chlorophyllous in nature with its figure.

Bread mould, *Amoeba*, *Aspergillus*, *Penicillium*, *Chlamydomonas*.

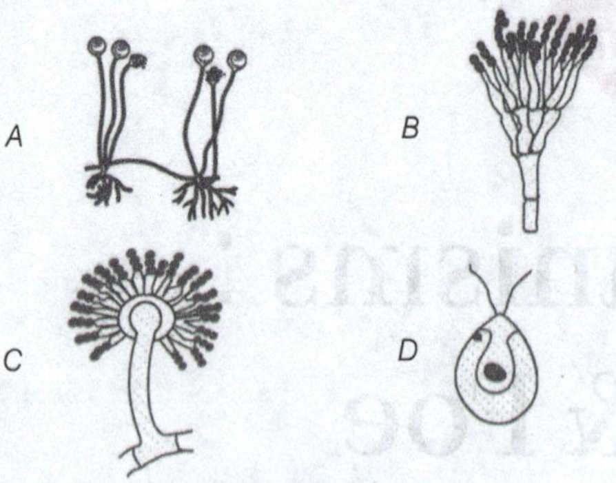

Mark the correct option.

(a) *A - Penicillium*
(b) *B - Amoeba*
(c) *C* - Bread mould
(d) *D - Chlamydomonas*

7. Match the microorganisms given in Column I to the group to which they belong given in Column II and choose the correct answer using the codes given below.

	Column I		Column II
A.	*Lactobacillus*	1.	Algae
B.	*Aspergillus*	2.	Protozoa
C.	*Spirogyra*	3.	Fungi
D.	*Paramecium*	4.	Bacteria

Codes

	A	B	C	D		A	B	C	D
(a)	4	3	1	2	(b)	1	2	4	3
(c)	4	1	2	3	(d)	3	2	1	4

8. Which of the following statements correctly corresponds to *Entamoeba?*

I. It is a single-celled microorganism.
II. It is classified as a plant.
III. It is classified as an animal.
IV. It is found in lakes, ponds and rivers.
V. It is found as internal parasite or commensals.

Choose the correct option.

(a) I and II
(b) I and III
(c) I, IV and V
(d) II and IV

9. Consider the statements given below.

I. *Paramecium* is a slipper-shaped Protozoa.
II. Foot and mouth diseases is a bacterial disease in animals.
III. Edward Jenner is the father of microbiology.
IV. *Aedes* mosquito is carriers of malaria.

Which of the above statements are incorrect?

(a) I, II and IV
(b) II, III and IV
(c) II, III and IV
(d) II and III

10. *X* in the figure can be identified as a fungal microorganism based on which of the following characteristics?

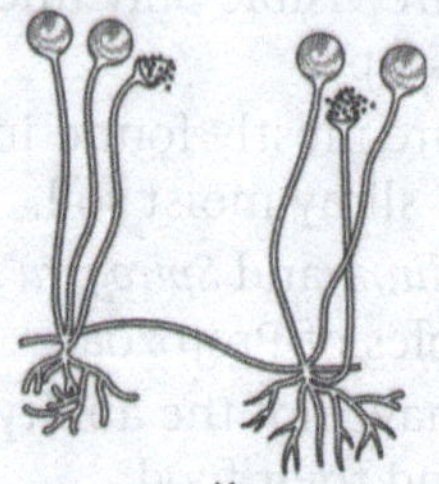

X

I. It is saprophyte organisms which reproduces through spores.
II. It is parasitic organisms which reproduces using host's body.

Choose the correct option.

(a) Statement II is correct
(b) Both statements I and II are correct
(c) Statement I is correct
(d) None of the above

11. Bacteria have been grouped into four different types based on their shapes. Identify the different types and select the correct statements regarding them.

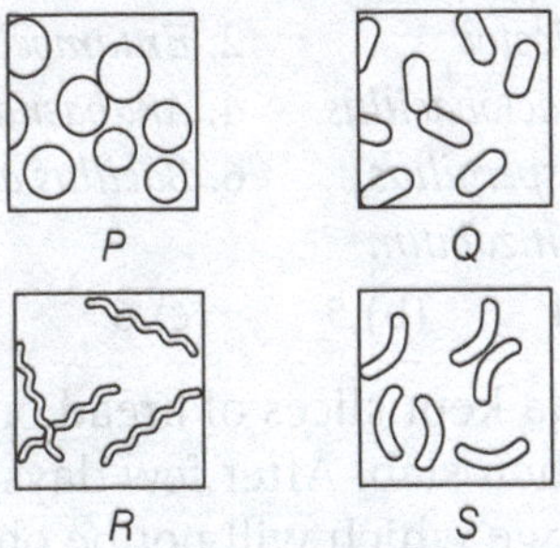

(a) *S* could be *Vibrio cholerae* which causes cholera in humans
(b) *Lactobacillus* could be an example of *P*, which helps in curdling of milk
(c) Type *R* bacteria are rod-shaped and called as bacilli
(d) Type *Q* bacteria are comma- shaped and are called as cocci bacteria

12. Observe the figures given below and identify the option which correctly pair the virus with its shape.

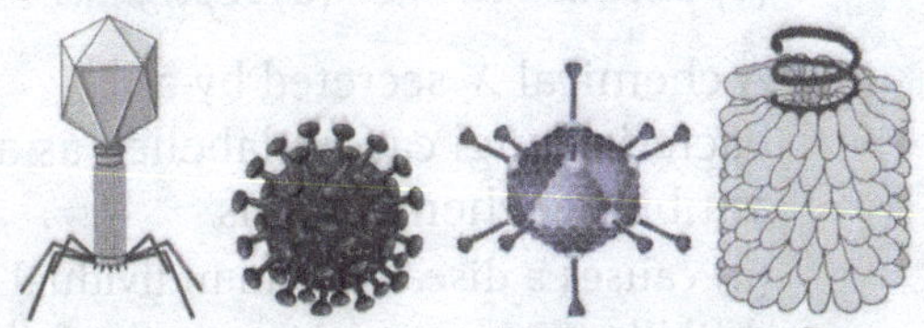

A. Bacteriophage virus   B. Influenza   C. Adenovirus   D. Tobacco mosaic virus

Mark the correct option.
(a) *A*- Complex   (b) *B* - Helical
(c) *C* - Spherical   (d) *D* - Polyhedral

13. Read the following statements about bacteria.
I. Bacteria are the unicellular organisms.
II. They have cell walls with defined nucleus.
III. They reproduce by binary fission and can grow very rapidly in favourable conditions.
IV. They can also reproduce sexually by exchanging genetic information through DNA or RNA.

Which of the above statement(s) is/are incorrect?
(a) I and IV
(b) Only II
(c) II and IV
(d) Only IV

14. Microorganisms *'X'* has been used for the large scale production of alcohol or wine. The process of conversion of sugar to alcohol is known as *'Y'*.
(a) *X-Penicillium*, *Y*-distillation
(b) *X*-Yeast, *Y*-fermentation
(c) *X-Lactobacillus*, *Y*-decantation
(d) *X-Streptococcus*, *Y*-decomposition

15. When fungal spores land on a piece of bread left on a table after a few days, the bread becomes mouldy. What conditions favour the growth of the fungus?
I. The presence of food.
II. The presence of moisture
III. The absence of water.
Choose the correct option.
(a) Only I
(b) Both I and II
(c) Both II and III
(d) I, II, III

16. Algae are used as food, as they are rich in carbohydrates, vitamins and few other inorganic substances. Which of the following can be considered as an example of such food?
(a) *Gelidium*
(b) *Spirogyra*
(c) *Rhodymenia*
(d) None of the above

17. Given below is a figure of a vector organism. Name the disease caused by it.

(a) Cholera (b) Malaria
(c) Hepatitis (d) Common cold

18. Given below is a list of diseases based on their insect vector. Pick the odd one out.

(a) Typhoid (b) Malaria
(c) Filariasis (d) Dengue

19. In which of the following groups only bacterial diseases are paired?

(a) Rabies, small pox, AIDS and malaria
(b) Anthrax, typhoid, hepatitis and cholera
(c) Typhoid, anthrax, tuberculosis and cholera
(d) Syphilis, AIDS, rabies and influenza

20. Match the items in Column I with preservatives used in Column II and choose the correct answer using the codes given below.

Column I (Items)	**Column II** (Preservatives used)
A. Meat	1. Hot and cold treatment
B. Jam and jellies	2. Common salt
C. Pickles	3. Sugar
D. Milk	4. Oil and vinegar

Codes

	A	B	C	D
(a)	4	2	1	3
(b)	2	3	4	1
(c)	2	1	3	4
(d)	1	2	4	3

21. Categorise the organisms given below as either friend or foe of humans. How many of them can be identified as beneficial for humans?

1. *Nostoc* 2. *Entamoeba*
3. *Lactobacillus* 4. *Anabaena*
5. *Aspergillus* 6. *Bacillus anthracis*
7. *Rhizobium*

(a) 4 (b) 5 (c) 6 (d) 3

22. Geeta kept slices of bread on the kitchen slab. After few days, the change which will not be observed in the spoiled bread is

(a) change in smell
(b) change in taste
(c) change in size
(d) change in colour

23. Some bacteria and fungi cause spoilage of food items. Which one is not responsible for food poisoning?

(a) Yeast (b) *Staphylococci*
(c) *Clostridium* (d) *Aspergillus*

24. A chemical *X* secreted by a bacteria/fungi can be labelled as an antibiotic when it can/is

(a) causes a disease in an individual
(b) kills or prevents the growth of bacteria in body
(c) produced as a result of a microorganism entering the body
(d) a protein made by WBCs which destroy microbes

25. Consider the statements given below.

I. Bread mould is a fungi.
II. Foot and mouth disease of cattle is caused by algae.
III. The bacterium which promotes the formation of curd is *Rhizobium*.
IV. The cyanobacteria commonly used as fertiliser is *Nostoc*.

Which of the above statements are incorrect?
(a) I and IV (b) II and III
(c) I, II and IV (d) I, II, III and IV

26. State (T) for True and (F) for False.
I. Anthrax is the common disease in humans and other animals.
II. Protozoa cause diseases like dysentery and malaria.
III. Edward Jenner discovered the process of fermentation.
IV. Jams, jellies and squashes are preserved by adding salt.

Codes

	I	II	III	IV
(a)	T	F	T	F
(b)	T	T	F	T
(c)	F	F	T	T
(d)	F	T	F	F

27. State (T) for True and (F) for False.
I. Protozoans feed on fungi and bacteria which are harmful to human beings.
II. Fungi are used in agriculture to enhance the fertility of soil.
III. Yeast produces CH_4 when it multiplies rapidly causing dough to rise.
IV. Citrus canker is a fungal disease transmitted through seeds.
V. Agar-agar is used in preparation of ice creams.

Codes

	I	II	III	IV	V
(a)	T	F	F	T	T
(b)	T	T	T	T	T
(c)	T	T	F	F	T
(d)	T	F	F	F	T

28. Observe and identify the process shown by the equation.

$$\text{Nitrogen} \xrightarrow{\text{Bacteria}} \text{Nitrates}$$

(a) Nitrification (b) Nitrogen-fixation
(c) Decomposition (d) Denitrification

29. Among the organisms mentioned below, which one is capable of fixing nitrogen while living symbiotically with the roots of leguminous plants?
(a) *Rhizobium* (b) *Pseudomonas*
(c) *Clostridium* (d) *Nostoc*

30. Match the Column I having the name of the microorganism with the characteristic given in Column II and choose the correct answer using the codes given below.

Column I (Microorganism)	Column II (Characteristic)
A. *Rhizobium*	1. Unicellular or multicellular
B. *Lactobacillus*	2. Nitrogen fixer
C. Virus	3. Malaria, dysentery
D. Protozoa	4. Disease causing microbe
E. Algae	5. Setting of curd

Codes

	A	B	C	D	E
(a)	3	5	4	2	1
(b)	1	3	2	5	4
(c)	4	3	5	1	2
(d)	2	5	4	3	1

31. The nitrogen gas of the atmosphere is converted into compounds of nitrogen to be used by the plants. Which of the following helps in the process?
A. By nitrogen-fixing bacteria in soil.
B. By earthworm.
C. By lightning.
D. By *Rhizobium* in root nodules.
E. By other microorganisms such as fungi.

Choose the correct option.
(a) A and B (b) B and C
(c) A, C, D and E (d) B and E

2 Marks Questions

32. Milk, if left out of the refrigerator will go sour and appear as shown below in the figure. Which of the following are incorrect regarding this figure?

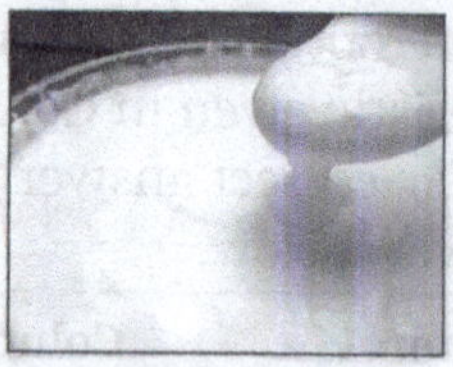

A. Viruses cause milk to go sour faster.

B. As milk goes sour, it becomes more acidic.

C. The higher the temperature, the faster the milk will go sour.

D. Bacterial action causes the milk to go sour.

E. Milk is converted into acetic acid.

Choose the option which indicates incorrect statements.

(a) A and B
(b) B and D
(c) A and E
(d) C and D

33. Match the following disease with its causative agents and choose the correct answer from the code given below.

	Name of disease		Causative agent
A.	Finrot	1.	Paramyxoviridae family's virus
B.	Botulism	2.	*Bacillus anthracis*
C.	Rinderpest	3.	Gram-negative bacteria
D.	Anthrax	4.	*Clostridium botulinum*

Codes

	A	B	C	D		A	B	C	D
(a)	3	2	1	4	(b)	2	1	3	4
(c)	1	2	4	3	(d)	3	4	1	2

34. Which of the following statements are correct regarding this figure given below?

Aspergillus

I. It is a bacterial microorganisms.

II. The group of diseases caused by this mould is referred to as aspergillosis.

III. The illness resulting from aspergillosis infection usually affect the respiratory system.

Choose the correct option.

(a) Statements I and II are correct
(b) Only statement III is correct
(c) Statements I, II and III are correct
(d) Statements II and III are correct

35. The figure given below shows the nitrogen cycle.

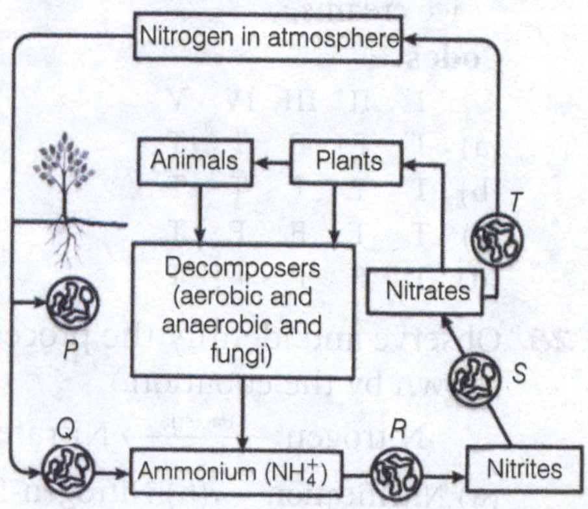

Identify the events taking place at *P*-*T* and select the correct option.

I. *P* → Symbiotic association of *Azospirillum*.

II. *Q* → Ammonification of atmospheric N_2.

III. *R* and *S* → Nitrification
i.e. $NH_4^+ \longrightarrow NO_3^-$

IV. *T* → Denitrification, i.e.
$NO_3^- \xrightarrow{Pseudomonas} NO_2^-$

Codes

(a) II, III and IV (b) III and IV
(c) I, II and IV (d) All of these

36. Given below is a list of general preventive measures.
Categorise them so as to given to the family of a patient who had been suffering from.

A. TB B. Cholera
C. Malaria

Preventive measures are

I. spray insecticides in homes.
II. eat properly cooked food.
III. patient should be kept in complete isolation.
IV. maintain personal hygiene.
V. drink clean and boiled drinking water.
VI. put fine wire mesh on doors and windows.

Select the appropriate option.

	A	B	C
(a)	II, I	III, IV	V, VI
(b)	III	II, IV, V	I, VI
(c)	I, VI	III, V	II, VI
(d)	I, II	III, IV	V, VI

Chapter 03

Coal and Petroleum

1 Mark Questions

1. Consider the following states of carbon.

I. Coke   II. Charcoal
III. Petrol   IV. Graphite

Which of these are considered as free states of carbon?

(a) I and II
(b) II and III
(c) I, II and III
(d) I, II and IV

2. I am a thick, black liquid with an unpleasant smell. I am a mixture of 200 substances. What am I ?

(a) Coke
(b) Coal
(c) Coal tar
(d) Coal gas

3. Consider the following statements about exhaustible natural resources.

Statement I Limited in quantity.

Statement II Not dependent on nature.

Statement III Exhausted by human activities.

The correct statements are

(a) I and II
(b) II and III
(c) I and III
(d) I, II and III

4. Match the distillation product of coal given in Column I with their preparation/applications given in Column II and choose the correct answer using the codes given below.

	Column I		Column II
A.	Coke	1.	Remains of vegetation
B.	Coal tar	2.	Fuel
C.	Coal gas	3.	Synthesis of plastics, paints, etc
D.	Coal	4.	Extraction of metals

Codes

	A	B	C	D
(a)	1	3	2	4
(b)	4	3	2	1
(c)	4	2	3	1
(d)	1	2	3	4

5. Which of the following are the incorrect set of fuel with their calorific value?

Fuel	Calorific value (kJ/g)
(a) Charcoal	35
(b) Coke	33
(c) Petrol	47
(d) LPG	90

6. Which of the following product is formed after complete combustion of methane?

(a) Carbon dioxide (b) Carbon monoxide
(c) Charcoal (d) Carbon

7. Match of the following from Column I with Column II.

Column I	Column II
A. Carbon dioxide	1. Coal, petroleum and natural gas
B. Air and water	2. Inexhaustible natural resource
C. Sun light	3. Natural resources
D. Fossil fuel	4. Burning of coal

Codes

	A	B	C	D		A	B	C	D
(a)	3	4	2	1	(b)	4	3	2	1
(c)	4	2	3	1	(d)	1	2	3	4

8. Consider the following actions while driving.

I. Switch OFF engine at traffic lights.
II. Ensure correct tyre pressure.
III. Maintain vehicle well from time to time.

Which will help in saving petrol?

(a) I and II (b) II and III
(c) Only III (d) I, II and III

9. State [T] for True and [F] for False.

I. Bitumen is obtained from coal tar.
II. Wildlife is an example of exhaustible natural resource.
III. Bitumen is used for surfacing roads.
VI. Carbonisation is a fast process.

Codes

	I	II	III	IV		I	II	III	IV
(a)	F	T	T	F	(b)	F	T	F	T
(c)	T	F	F	T	(d)	T	F	T	F

10. Rohan saw a bucket filled with some black liquid. When he went near the liquid, he felt some unpleasant odour. The engineer working there tell him that this substance is a mixture of 200 substances.

On the basis of information provided above, could you guess what was that substance?

(a) Coke (b) Coal
(c) Coal tar (d) Coal gas

11. Consider the given figure of destructive distillation of coal and identify the *A*, *B* and *C*.

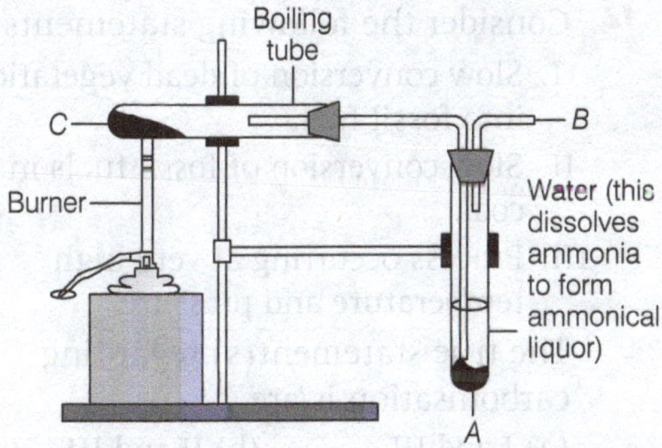

	A	*B*	*C*
(a)	Coal tar	Coal gas	Powered coke
(b)	Coal gas	Coal tar	Powered coke
(c)	Coal tar	Powdered gas	Coal gas
(d)	Powdered gas	Coal tar	Coal gas

12. Coal is processed in industries to get some useful products. Some products that are supposed to be obtained from the coal are

I. Coke II. Coal gas
III. Coal tar IV. CNG

The correct products are

(a) I and II (b) I and III
(c) I, II and III (d) I, II, III and IV

13. Substance *X* is obtained by processing coal and was used for street lighting in 1810 or 1820. It is used for the preparation of

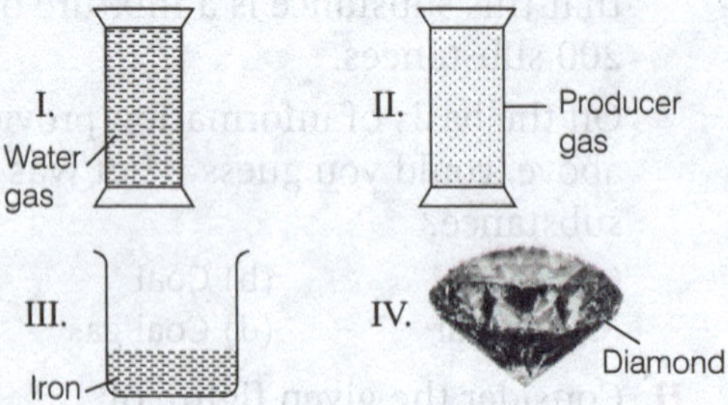

(a) I and II (b) I, II and IV
(c) I, III and IV (d) Only IV

14. Consider the following statements.

I. Slow conversion of dead vegetation into fossil fuel.
II. Slow conversion of fossil fuels into coal.
III. Process occurring at very high temperature and pressure.

The true statement(s) regarding carbonisation is/are

(a) I and III (b) II and III
(c) Only I (d) Only III

15. Several materials can be obtained from coal tar, some of them are mentioned below.

I. Naphthalene balls
II. Perfumes
III. Drugs
IV. Cookware
V. Fuel
VI. Extracted metal

The correct materials are

(a) I and III
(b) I, II and III
(c) II, III and IV
(d) III, IV and VI

16. Complete the following sentence by selecting the most appropriate set of words.

X is a type of coal which contains around *Y*% of carbon and it is also known as *Z* coal.

	X	*Y*	*Z*
(a)	Lignite	86%	black
(b)	Lignite	60%	brown
(c)	Bituminous	86%	black
(d)	Bituminous	60%	brown

17. Consider the following types of coal

I. Peat
II. Lignite
III. Bituminous
IV. Anthracite

Which of the following has/have brown colour?

(a) I and II (b) II and III
(c) I and III (d) I, II, III and IV

18. Match the varieties of coal given in Column I with their carbon content/property given in Column II and choose the correct alternative using the codes given below.

Column I	Column II
A. Lignite	1. Most common variety
B. Anthracite	2. 60% carbon
C. Peat	3. 30% carbon
D. Bituminous	4. Purest variety
	5. Brown coal

Codes

	A	B	C	D		A	B	C	D
(a)	5	4	2	1	(b)	5	4	3	1
(c)	4	1	2	3	(d)	5	1	3	4

19. In homework Seeta's teacher gave assignment for writing one word for the following observation/sentences.

I. It is a best alternative to petrol and diesel in vehicles.
II. The major component of LPG.
III. The petroleum product is used for metalling the roads in place of coal tar.

Could you help Seeta in identifying, I II and III?

	I	II	III
(a)	CNG	Butane	Bitumen
(b)	Hydrogen fuel	Butane	Peat
(c)	CNG	Propane	Bitumen
(d)	Hydrogen fuel	Propane	Bitumen

20. In homework, Ravi's teacher gave him an assignment for writing one word for the following substances.

I. A mixture of about 200 substances.
II. A porous, black, almost pure form of carbon.
III. A fossil fuel used in thermal power plants for generating electricity.

Could you help Ravi in identifying I, II and III?

	I	II	III
(a)	Coke	Coal gas	Petroleum
(b)	Coal tar	Coke	Coal
(c)	Coke	Coal tar	Coal
(d)	Coal tar	Coal	Coal gas

21. Which of the following sources of energy can be a good alternative of coal in a power station?

I. Geothermal energy
II. Energy from water
III. Energy from petrol
IV. Energy from plants

Codes

(a) I and II (b) 1,II and III
(c) Only IV (d) 1, II, III and IV

22. Consider the following statements.

I. Coal is made up of only carbon.
II. Anthracite and lignite are the two main types of coal.
III. Anthracite coal is the hardest and has more çarbon content.
IV. Lignite is the softest and has high carbon and oxygen content.

The incorrect statements are

(a) I and III
(b) 1,II and II
(c) I, II and IV
(d) II, III and IV

23. State [T] for True and [F] for False.

I. Coal is a non-renewable resource.
II. Anthracite coal is the hardest and has more carbon.
III. Oxygen in air is an exhaustible natural resource.
IV. Coal is a fossil fuel and it is as hard as stone.

Codes

	I	II	III	IV		I	II	III	IV
(a)	T	T	F	T	(b)	T	T	T	F
(c)	T	F	T	F	(d)	F	F	T	T

24. Petroleum is deposited with gas in the rocks known as oil wells from where it is taken out by drilling.

In these wells, the petroleum and gas are found in the layer *X*-water because they are *Y*-than water.

	X	*Y*
(a)	Below	Heavier
(b)	Above	Lighter
(c)	Between	Of equal weight
(d)	Similar to	Of equal weight

25. Consider the following statements about natural gas.

I. It is difficult to transport it through pipes.
II. It cannot be used directly for burning in homes.
III. It is stored under high pressure as compressed natural gas.
IV. It cannot be used for power generation.

The incorrect statements are

(a) I and II (b) III and IV
(c) I, II and III (d) I, II and IV

26. Match the items given in Column I with the items given in Column II and choose the correct answer using the codes given below.

Column I	Column II
A. Petroleum gas in liquid form	1. Black gold
B. Natural gas	2. LPG
C. Petroleum	3. CNG
D. Paraffin wax	4. Bitumen
	5. Vaseline

Codes

	A	B	C	D		A	B	C	D
(a)	2	3	1	4	(b)	4	3	1	5
(c)	2	3	1	5	(d)	3	2	5	1

27. Consider the following statements.

I. Carbon monoxide is a colourless, odourless and tasteless gas.
II. The oxides of sulphur and nitrogen are released when coal is burnt.
III. Natural gas consists mainly of methane.
IV. The calorific value of petrol is 97.

The correct statements are

(a) I and II (b) I, II and III
(c) I, II and IV (d) I, III and IV

28. Which of the following are the constituents of petroleum?

(a) Diesel, paraffin
(b) CNG, coal tar
(c) Coal tar, bitumen
(d) Kerosene, coal gas

29. Match the Column I with Column II.

Column I (Fuel)	Column II (Calorific value)
A. Coal	1. 48
B. Methane	2. 45
C. Diesel	3. 55
D. Kerosene	4. 25-33

Codes

	A	B	C	D		A	B	C	D
(a)	1	2	3	4	(b)	3	2	4	1
(c)	4	2	3	1	(d)	4	3	2	1

30. Match the Column I with Column II.

Column I	Column II
A. Petrol	1. Used in ointments and vaseline
B. Kerosene	2. Fuel for light vehicles
C. Diesel	3. Fuel in lamps
D. Paraffin wax	4. Fuel for heavy vehicles

Codes

	A	B	C	D		A	B	C	D
(a)	2	3	4	1	(b)	2	3	1	4
(c)	4	3	2	1	(d)	3	2	1	4

31. Consider the following statements about an ideal fuel.

I. It should have a high calorific value.
II. It should have high rate of combustion.
III. It should not cause pollution on burning.
IV. It should release heat in uncontrolled manner.

The incorrect statements are

(a) I and II (b) II and IV
(c) I and III (d) I, II and III

32. State [T] for True and [F] for false.

I. Petroleum is found in pure form under the sand.
II. Paraffin wax is a petrochemical.
III. LPG produces carbon dioxide gas on burning.
IV. Petroleum is soluble in water.

Codes

	I	II	III	IV		I	II	III	IV
(a)	T	T	F	F	(b)	F	T	F	T
(c)	F	T	T	F	(d)	F	T	F	F

33. When subjected to fractional distillation, petroleum gives different fractions, some of which are mentioned below.

I. Petroleum gas
II. Lubricating oil
III. Kerosene
IV. Gasoline

What is the correct sequence of these fractions in the fractionating column from top to bottom?

(a) I, II, III, IV (b) III, I, II, IV
(c) I, IV, III, II (d) IV, III, I, II

34. State [T] for True and [F] for False.

I. Natural gas can be supplied to homes and factories through pipes.
II. Natural gas is obtained by fractional distillation of crude oil.
III. Natural gas is a cleaner fuel because on burning only water is produced.
IV. Natural gas is an exhaustible source of energy like fossil fuels.

Codes

	I	II	III	IV		I	II	III	IV
(a)	T	F	T	T	(b)	T	T	F	T
(c)	F	T	T	F	(d)	F	F	T	F

35. State [T] for True and [F] for False

I. The ignition temperature of an ideal fuel should be low.
II. The calorific value of hydrogen is 150 kJ/g.
III. Charcoal is the example of solid fuel.
IV. Anthracite contains around 60% of carbon.

Codes

	I	II	III	IV		I	II	III	IV
(a)	T	T	F	F	(b)	T	T	T	F
(c)	F	T	F	T	(d)	T	F	T	F

36. Consider the following statements.

I. During the fractional distillation of petroleum, hydrocarbons having highest boiling point condenses first.
II. Petrochemicals are those useful substances that are obtained from petroleum and natural gas.
III. Paraffin wax is used in making candles, vaseline, polish, etc.

The correct statements are

(a) I and II (b) II and III
(c) I and III (d) I,II and III

37. When petroleum is subjected to fractional distillation, a fraction X, lies in between the petrol and diesel oil is obtained. This fraction is used

I. as a fuel for stoves and lamps.
II. in paints and motor fuel.
III. in jet fuel.

The correct use (s) is/are

(a) I and II (b) I and III
(c) II and III (d) Only I

2 Marks Questions

38. Complete the following sentence by selecting the most appropriate set of words.

X is an exhaustible natural resource which is found in *Y* quantity in nature and is *Z* likely to get exhausted by human activities.

	X	*Y*	*Z*
(a)	Coal	limited	always
(b)	Air	unlimited	most
(c)	Sunlight	unlimited	never
(d)	Petroleum	unlimited	never

39. Coal is a fossil fuel and it cannot be prepared in the laboratory or industry because its preparation

I. is a very slow process.

II. occurs only at a very low temperature and pressure.

III. requires very high temperature and pressure.

IV. is a great source of pollution.

The correct reasons are

(a) I and II (b) II and IV

(c) I and III (d) II, I and IV

40. Consider the following statements.

I. Oil and natural gas are found under the ground between folds of rock in the porous areas.

II. In search of oil and natural gas, companies drill through the earth to the deposits deep below the surface.

III. The oil and natural gas are then pumped from the ground by oil rigs.

IV. The petroleum or crude oil can be used in the same state in which it is found.

The correct statements are

(a) I and II

(b) I, II and III

(c) II, III and IV

(d) II and II

41. Consider the following statements about uses of different components of petroleum.

Statement I Diesel used as a fuel for engines and generators.

Statement II Petrol used as a solvent for dry cleaning.

Statement III Kerosene is used as a fuel for stoves.

The correct statements are

(a) I and II

(b) II and III

(c) I and III

(d) I, II and III

42. State [T] for True and [F] for False.

I. Wildlife is an exhaustible natural resource.

II. Methane is released during mining of coal.

III. Fossil fuels should be conserved because they give out lots of heat.

IV. Resources that are present in unlimited quantity in nature are called exhaustible natural resources.

V. Burning of coal in insufficient amount of oxygen results in the formation of carbon dioxide.

Codes

	I	II	III	IV	V
(a)	T	T	F	T	F
(b)	F	T	T	F	F
(c)	T	T	F	F	F
(d)	T	F	F	F	F

Chapter

04

Combustion and Flame

1 Mark Questions

1. Combustion takes place only when

I. oxygen/air is available.

II. air/oxygen and fuel are available.

III. temperature of the fuel is lower than ignition temperature.

IV. temperature of the fuel is above the ignition temperature.

The correct statements are

(a) I and II (b) II and IV

(c) I and III (d) I and IV

2. Some combustible and non-combustible materials are listed below in the box.

Charcoal, chalk, stone, iron rod, copper coin, straw, cardboard, glass paper, candle, wood.

How many of the following can be considered as combustible?

(a) 4 (b) 5 (c) 6 (d) 7

3. Some processes are given below

I. Burning of candle

II. Burning of wood

III. Burning of paper

From these, the example(s) of slow combustion is/are

(a) Only II (b) Only III

(c) II and III (d) I, II and III

4. Consider the following experiment,

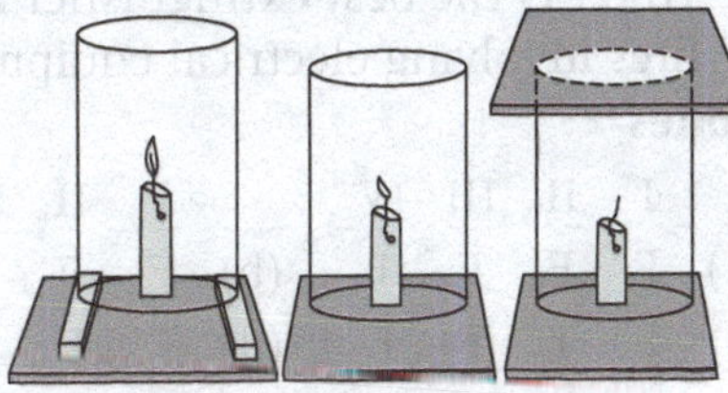

(A) (B) (C)

This experiment shows that

(a) candle can burn in a glass chimney

(b) candle cannot burn in a glass chimney

(c) wood is essential for combustion

(d) oxygen is essential for combustion

5. Mayank was cooking kaju curry on a chulha. To his surprise, he observed that the copper vessel was getting blackened from outside. It may be due to

(a) proper combustion of fuel

(b) improper cooking of kaju curry

(c) improper combustion of the fuel

(d) burning of copper vessel

6. Consider the following statements,

I. Sulphur burns in air at room temperature.

II. Most fires occur due to human carelessness.

III. During rapid combustion, a material suddenly bursts into flame.

IV. Spontaneous combustion of coal dust has led to forest fires.

The correct statements are

(a) I and II (b) II and III
(c) II and IV (d) II and IV

7. State [T] for True [F] for False.

I. Magnesium is a non-combustible metal.
II. Calorific value of wood is higher than that of coal.
III. A physical process in which a substance reacts with oxygen to given off heat is called combustion.
IV. Water is the best extinguisher for fires involving electrical equipment.

Codes

	I	II	III	IV		I	II	III	IV
(a)	F	F	F	T	(b)	F	F	T	F
(c)	F	T	F	F	(d)	F	F	F	F

8. Consider the following diagram.

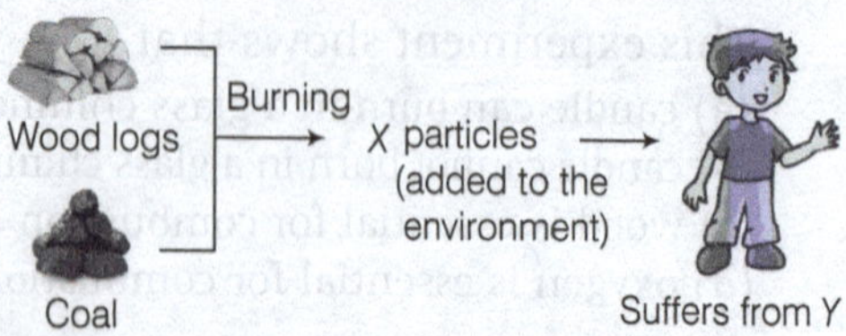

Here, *X* and *Y* are

(a) burnt carbon, respiratory disease
(b) burnt carbon, nervous disease
(c) únburnt carbon, respiratory disease
(d) unburnt carbon, stomach disease

9. Some cooking oil caught fire in the kitchen. She put water to extinguish it but the fire was not put off. The oil continued to burn. Why?

I. Oil is lighter than water.
II. Water sinks while oil stays on the top and keeps burning.
III. Oil sinks while water stays on the top and keeps burning.

Choose the correct option.

(a) Both I and III (b) Both II and III
(c) Only I (d) Both I and II

10. Match the processes given in Column I with their combustion type given in Column II and choose the correct answer using the codes given below.

Column I	Column II
A. Burning of candle	1. Explosion
B. Burning of phosphorus	2. Slow combustion
C. Burning of LPG	3. Incomplete combustion
D. Burning of crackers	4. Spontaneous combustion
	5. Rapid combustion

Codes

	A	B	C	D		A	B	C	D
(a)	2	3	4	1	(b)	2	4	3	1
(c)	2	4	5	1	(d)	2	4	1	5

11. Sarthak had a matchstick he was lighting it suddenly his clothes caught fire, the best way to extinguish the fire is to

(a) throw water on the clothes
(b) use fire extinguisher
(c) cover the person with a woollen blanket
(d) cover the person with a polythene sheet

12. State [T] for True and [F] for False and choose the correct option.

I. Fire extinguishers extinguish the fire by bringing down the temperature of fuel.
II. The heat and light produced by Sun are also the result of combustion process.

III. Fire can be controlled by removing one or more factors essential for its production.
IV. Ignition temperature is very low for inflammable substances.

Codes

	I	II	III	IV		I	II	III	IV
(a)	F	F	T	T	(b)	T	T	F	F
(c)	F	T	T	F	(d)	F	F	F	T

13. Consider the following figures.

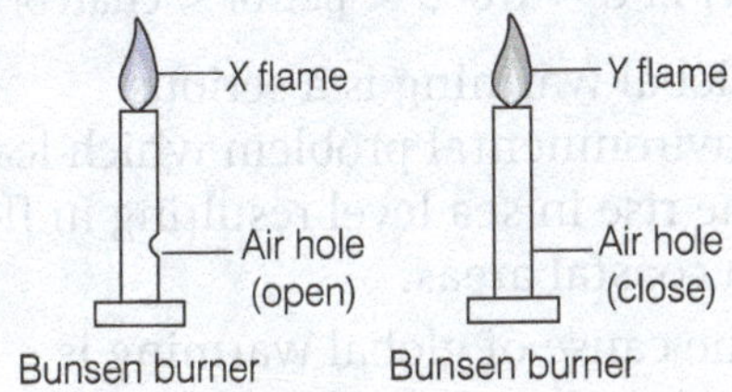

Here, *X* and *Y* respectively are
(a) blue and green (b) yellow and blue
(c) yellow and green (d) blue and yellow

14. Rajni wondered why a flame always points upwards. This is because
(a) the gases produced in a flame are hot
(b) hot gases are light and rise up
(c) cold gases are formed in the flame
(d) Both (a) and (b)

15. State [T] for True and [F] for False.
I. In luminous zone of a candle, partial combustion takes place with the evolution of large quantity of heat energy.
II. Middle zone is the hottest part of the flame.
III. All the fuels burn with flame.
IV. Kerosene oil and molten wax produce flame.

Codes

	I	II	III	IV		I	II	III	IV
(a)	F	T	T	F	(b)	F	F	T	F
(c)	F	T	T	T	(d)	F	F	F	T

16. State [T] for True and [F] for False.
I. Charcoal vapourise and so produce a flame.
II. Blue flame does not produce much light, so it is said to be a luminous flame.
III. Goldsmith uses the middle zone of the flame for melting gold and silver
IV. Due to the absence of air, the flame flickers and produces smoke.

Codes

	I	II	III	IV		I	II	III	IV
(a)	F	F	F	T	(b)	T	F	F	F
(c)	F	T	F	F	(d)	F	T	T	F

17. Ramesh wants to test the hotness of different parts of the flame. For this, he took a beaker filled with water and heat it in
I. non-luminous zone.
II. dark zone.
III. luminous zone.

He recorded the time taken by the same amount of water to reach a temperature of 50°C and make the following table.

Zone	Volume of water taken	Time taken to reach 50°C
I.	20 mL	15 min
II.	20 mL	10 min
III.	20 mL	20 min

The incorrect observation(s) is/are
(a) Only III (b) II and III
(c) Only II (d) Only I

18. In case of good fuels, ignition temperature is *X* and calorific value is *Y*. *X* and *Y* respectively are
(a) low and high (b) low and low
(c) high and low (d) high and high

19. Match the pollutants given in Column I with their harmful effects given in Column II and choose the correct answer using the codes given below.

Column I	Column II
A. Smoke	1. Greenhouse effect
B. Carbon monoxide	2. Lung diseases
C. Dust	3. Allergic reaction
D. Oxides of nitrogen	4. Chocking of throat
	5. Respiratory problems

Codes

	A	B	C	D
(a)	5	3	2	1
(b)	5	4	3	2
(c)	4	3	2	1
(d)	5	3	4	2

20. Match the items of Column I with the items of Column II and choose the correct answer using the codes given below.

Column I	Column II
A. Oxides of sulphur and nitrogen	1. Incomplete combustion of coal
B. Oxygen	2. Acid rain
C. Carbon dioxide	3. Necessary for combustion
D. Carbon monoxide	4. Fire extinguisher

Codes

	A	B	C	D		A	B	C	D
(a)	4	2	3	1	(b)	1	2	3	4
(c)	2	3	4	1	(d)	4	3	2	1

21. In an experiment, 4.5 kg of a fuel was completely burnt. During this process, the heat produced was 180000 kJ. The calorific value of the fuel (in kJ/kg) is

(a) 10000 (b) 20000
(c) 40000 (d) 80000

22. The correct increasing order of calorific value of the given combustible substances

(a) Wood < charcoal < petrol < LPG
(b) Wood < LPG < petrol < charcoal
(c) Petrol < wood < LPG < charcoal
(d) LPG < wood < petrol < charcol

23. Global warming is a serious environmental problem which leads to the rise in sea level resulting in floods in coastal areas.

The cause of global warming is

(a) sulphur dioxide released by combustion of fuels and resulting in increased temperature
(b) carbon monoxide added to the environment due to combustion of fuel and result in decreased temperature
(c) carbon dioxide added to the environment due to combustion of fuel and resulting in increased temperature
(d) None of the above

24. The clearing of forest is called *X* and this can cause the soil to be washed away in a process called soil *Y*. The excess carbon dioxide in the air results in *Z*.

What can *X*, *Y* and *Z* be?

	X	*Y*	*Z*
(a)	Deforestation	Erosion	Global warming
(b)	Deforestation	Degradation	Heating
(c)	Logging	Erosion	Cooling
(d)	Logging	Degradation	Global warming

25. In severe cold weather, Mayank's family burnt wood in the room during the night keeping the windows close. After sometime they felt suffocation . Mayank immediately opened the windows and get relief what did actually happen?

(a) Due to the formation of carbon monoxide which is a highly poisonous gas. It causes suffocation in closed room.
(b) Due to the formation of carbon dioxide which is a highly poisonous gas. It causes suffocation in closed room.
(c) Due to the formation of sulphur dioxide which is a highly poisonous gas. It causes suffocation in closed room
(d) None of the above

26. Consider the consequences of green house effect.

I. Existence of life on the Earth.
II. Melting of ice on the Earth's pole.
III. Floods on low lying areas of the Earth.
IV. Warmth of the Earth.

The correct statements are
(a) I and IV
(b) II and III
(c) I, II and III
(d) All of the above

27. If *A* is hydrogen, which property of *A* prevents it from becoming an ideal fuel?

(a) Its highest calorific value
(b) Its very low ignition temperature
(c) Its very high solubility in water
(d) Its pollution free nature as the byproduct formed after combustion is also important for existence of life.

28. In the following venn diagram,

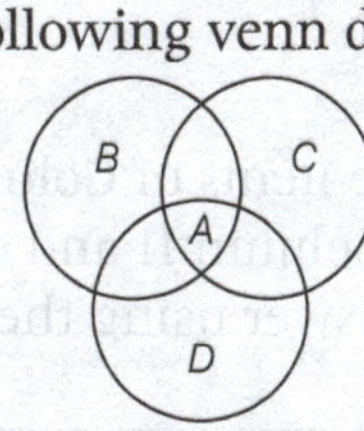

Identify *A*, *B*, *C* and *D*.

	A	*B*	*C*	*D*
(a)	Natural fuels	Wood	Coal	Cowdung cake
(b)	Fossil fuels	Wood	Coal	Petroleum
(c)	Natural fuels	Petroleum	Wood	Coal
(d)	Fossil fuels	Cowdung cake	Wood	Petroleum

29. Ramesh has bought a new auto. Suggest a fuel that pollutes the environment the least and is also economical.

(a) LPG (b) Petrol
(c) CNG (d) Diesel

30. Ankit takes three watch glasses containing milk, petrol and mustard oil respectively. Suppose he bring a burning candle near these materials one by one, which materials will catch fire instantly?

(a) The watch glass containing petrol
(b) The watch glass containing milk
(c) The watch glass containing mustard oil
(d) The watch glasses containing petrol and mustard oil.

2 Marks Questions

31. Match the items of Column I with the items of Column II and choose the correct answer using the codes given below.

Column I	Column II
A. LPG	1. Non-combustible
B. Iron nails	2. Deforestation
C. Candle	3. Cooking gas
D. Wood	4. Flame

Codes

	A	B	C	D		A	B	C	D
(a)	1	2	3	4	(b)	3	2	4	1
(c)	4	3	2	1	(d)	3	4	2	1

32. Sometimes, rainwater is found harmful for crops, buildings, soil, etc. Such rain is called acid rain and is responsible for the decolouration of Taj Mahal over years. The main cause of acid rain is

(a) release of carbon monoxide due to incomplete combustion of fuel, which dissolves in rainwater to give acid rain

(b) release of carbon particles in the atmosphere which dissolve in rainwater to give acid rain

(c) release of oxides of sulphur and nitrogen during the combustion of fuel, which dissolve in rainwater to give acid rain

(d) release of methane and other gases due to burning of wood, which dissolve in rainwater to give acid rain

33. State [T] for True and [F] for False.

I. Magnesium is a non-combustible metal.

II. A physical process in which a substance reacts with oxygen to give off heat is called combustion.

III. Alcohol, CNG and LPG are inflammable substances.

IV. Carbon dioxide is an excellent fire extinguisher.

V. At airport and petrol pump, soda-acid fire extinguishers are not used.

Codes

	I	II	III	IV	V
(a)	F	F	T	F	T
(b)	F	F	T	T	T
(c)	F	T	T	T	F
(d)	T	F	F	T	T

34. State [T] for True and [F] for False.

I. Increased concentration of nitrogen in air is believed to cause global warming.

II. A good fuel is one which does not burn.

III. The use of diesel and petrol as fuels is being replaced by CNG.

IV. Kerosene is an example of a liquid fuel.

Codes

	I	II	III	IV		I	II	III	IV
(a)	F	F	T	T	(b)	F	T	T	F
(c)	F	F	F	T	(d)	T	F	F	T

35. When a candle burns in air, following two changes take place.

Change *A* and change *B*.

Some of the statements about change *A* and change *B* are given below.

I. Change *A* is a chemical change.

II. Change *B* is a reversible change.

III. Both change *A* and change *B* are irreversible.

The correct statement(s) is/are

(a) Only I (b) I and II

(c) I and III (d) Only III

36. Match the following for the flame of a candle choose the correct answer.

Column I	Column II (Zone)	Column III (Colour)
A. Hottest part	1. Innermost zone of unburnt wax vapours	(*X*) Blue
B. Moderately hot	2. Middle zone of partial combustion	(*Y*) Black
C. Least hot	3. Outer zone of complete combustion	(*Z*) Yellow

Codes

(a) A - 3 - *X*, B - 2 - *Z*, C - 1 - *Y*
(b) A - 2 - *X*, B - 1 - *Z*, C - 2 - *Y*
(c) A - 3 - *Y*, B - 2 - *X*, C - 1 - *Z*
(d) A - 2 - *Z*, B - 1 - *Y*, C - 2 - *X*

37. Match the items given in Column I with their most suitable match given in Column II and choose the correct answer using the codes given below.

Column I	Column II
A. Rapid combustion	1. Material burns without any apparent cause.
B. Explosion	2. Fire extinguishers.
C. Baking soda	3. Material burns with only sound but no heat or light.
D. Spontaneous combustion	4. Evolution of large amount of heat, light and sound.
	5. Material burns rapidly to give heat and light.

Codes

	A	B	C	D		A	B	C	D
(a)	5	4	1	2	(b)	5	4	2	1
(c)	5	3	2	1	(d)	4	5	1	3

Chapter 05

Conservation of Plants and Animals

1 Mark Questions

1. Animal *X* is at an extremely high risk of becoming extinct. Such animals are labelled in Red Data Book as

(a) endangered
(b) vulnerable
(c) extinct
(d) critically endangered

2. Identify the incorrectly matched pair of protected areas and the species being protected

(a) Jim Corbett National Park—Tigers
(b) Kaziranga National Park—Tigers
(c) Gir National Park—Asiatic Lion
(d) Mudumalai Sanctuary—Indian elephant

3. Which of the following figure is wrongly mentioned?

(a) 
Endemic

(b) 
Extinct

(c) 
Threatened

(d) 
Endangered

4. In some countries, the buying and selling of animals such as orangutans and leatherback turtles have been banned. These animals need to be protected so that

(a) their value can increase
(b) their numbers can increase
(c) the zoos can attract more visitors
(d) scientists can have more animals for experiments

5. I was a large heavy flightless bird. I was hunted in large number in the island of Madagascar. The last member of my species died in 1680, who am I?

(a) Broad billed duck
(b) Dodo
(c) The great Indian bustard
(d) Grey jungle fowl

6. Would a city like Mumbai be greatly affected by deforestation? What would be the effects of deforestation on a large urban city?

(a) No, it would not be affected, it is too far from the forests
(b) Yes, it would be affected, there would be scarcity of water and resources got from forests, air pollution would also increase
(c) No, cities are independent and do not need forests for any purpose
(d) Yes, animals who have lost their habitat would come to the cities in search of food

7. Read the characteristics of two methods of biodiversity conservation.

P	*Q*
• A man-made place for animals.	• Animals live in their natural habitat. It is not man-made.
• The animals arc kept in artificial setting instead of their natural habitat and provided protection.	• It provides protection and suitable living conditions to wild animals just like in their natural habitat.

Select the option which correctly identifies *P* and *Q*.

	P	*Q*
(a)	Wildlife sanctuary	Biosphere reserve
(b)	Zoo	National parks
(c)	Zoo	Wildlife sanctuary
(d)	Wildlife sanctuary	Botanical gardens

8. Read the given statements and select the correct option.

Statement I A plant or animal species which is exclusively found in a particular area and is not found naturally anywhere else, is known as endemic species.

Statement II The existence of endemic species is often threatened due to the introduction of exotic species from some other geographical area.

(a) Both statements I and II are correct
(b) Both statements I and II are incorrect
(c) Statement I is correct and statement II is incorrect
(d) Statement I is incorrect and statement II is correct

9. Which of these actions should be adopted by us to save the environment?

I. We can plant trees in open spaces, parks and alongside road.
II. We can recycle our organic waste from kitchen for making compost and use it in our kitchen garden for growing plants.
III. We can save, reuse and recycle paper.
IV. We can keep birds and animals in our house.

Choose the correct option.

(a) I, II and IV
(b) I, II and III
(c) I, III and IV
(d) I, II, III and IV

2 Marks Questions

10. Which of the following is not a consequence of deforestation in an area?

I. Increase in CO_2 levels.
II. Increased rainfall.
III. Increase in groundwater levels.
IV. Soil erosion.
V. Habitat destruction.
VI. Increased temperature and pollution.
VII. Decreased flood and droughts.
VIII. Desertification.

Codes

(a) I, II and III (b) IV, V and VIII
(c) II, III and VII (d) I, IV, V, VI and VIII

11. Migratory birds like Siberian cranes fly to far away areas like Bharatpur sanctuary in Rajasthan every year during a particular time.

Which of the following conditions of their habitats is responsible for migratory habits of birds?

I. Unavailability of food.
II. Extremely cold weather conditions.
III. Lack of nesting (egg laying) areas.
IV. Overcrowding of their habitats.

Codes

(a) I and II (b) II and III
(c) III and IV (d) I, II and IV

12. Project Tiger is an initiative for tiger conservation, started in 1972-73 in India. From the box given below, identify the names associated with this project.

Sunderbans, Bharatpur sanctuary, Manas sanctuary, Bandipur National Park, Great Himalayan National Park, Jim Corbett National Park, Indian Botanical Garden.

Select the correct option.

(a) 4 (b) 5 (c) 3 (d) 2

13. Arrange in order, the process that leads to desertification.

(a) Soil erosion → fewer trees → removal of top layer of soil → less fertility, less humus → desertification
(b) Fewer trees → removal of top layer of soil → less fertility, less humus → soil erosion → desertification
(c) Removal of top layer of soil → fewer trees → soil erosion → less fertility, less humus → desertification
(d) Fewer trees → soil erosion → removal of top layer of soil → less fertility, less humus → desertification

14. The given below organism is not found in present era but many skeletons or fossils of these animals are found in different places of Earth providing an evidence that they were present on the Earth thousands of years ago.

What would be the reason/s that these organisms have disappeared from the world?

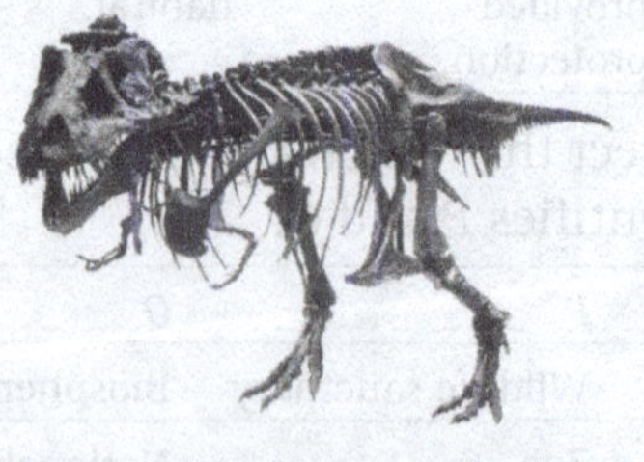

I. These animals were threatened or killed by other animals in abundance.
II. They were dependent on other organisms for their food.
III. The environmental conditions made their survival harder on Earth.
IV. They were not herbivores.

Select the correct option.

(a) Only I (b) Only II
(c) III and IV (d) II and III

Chapter

06

Reproduction in Animals

1 Mark Questions

1. In which part of the female reproductive system does a fertilised egg normally develop into a baby?

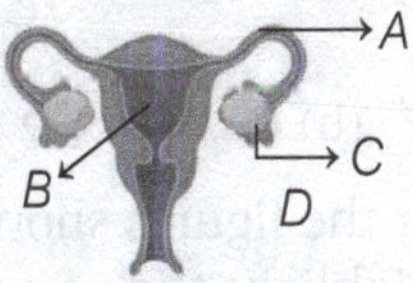

(a) *C* (b) *A* (c) *D* (d) *B*

2. Which one of the following is correct route for passage of sperms?

(a) Testes – Scrotum – Vas deferens – Urethra – Penis

(b) Scrotum – Testes – Urethra – Vas deferens – Penis

(c) Testes – Vas deferens – Urethra – Seminal vesicles

(d) Testes– Vas deferens – Urethra – Penis

3. The newborn baby will be a male or female depends upon the type of the combination of sex chromosomes. The type of sex chromosomes present in humans are *X* and *Y*.

Which of the following combination given below will give birth to *P* (male)…… and *Q* (female)……… ?

Codes

(a) *P* – XY, *Q* – XX (b) *P* – Y, *Q* – X
(c) *P* – XX, *Q* – XY (d) *P* – X, *Q* – Y

4. Given below is the information about the type of reproduction taking place in animal *X*.

I. Female organism lays hundreds of eggs in water.

II. Male partner deposits sperm over eggs.

III. Fertilisation takes place in water.

Animal *X* can most likely be

(a) starfish

(b) crocodile

(c) hens

(d) ostrich

5. Study the table shown below,

	In human
Female reproductive cell	*X*
Male reproductive cell	*Y*
Type of fertilisation	Internal
Post-fertilisation structure	*Z*

X, *Y* and *Z* are correctly identified as

	X	*Y*	*Z*
(a)	Ovule	Sperm	Embryo
(b)	Stigma	Pollen	Endosperm
(c)	Ova	Sperm	Zygote
(d)	Sperm	Ova	Zygote

6. Read the statements given below made by three children about reproduction.

I. **Joan** All living beings need an egg and a sperm to reproduce.

II. **Kate** Reproduction is way to prevent the extinction of a species.

III. **Belle** To ensure a higher chance of survival, all living things produce more than one offspring at a time.

Who made a correct statements?

(a) Kate only
(b) Joan and Kate
(c) Belle only
(d) Joan, Kate and Belle

7. Read the statements given below carefully. Identify the statements which are true and choose the correct option.

(a) The process of change by which a larva is transformed into an adult is called metamorphosis.
(b) The young ones look similar to the parents in animals that undergo metamorphosis.
(c) The stages in life cycle of a silkworm are egg → pupa → caterpillar → adult
(d) A tadpole is adapted to live on land whereas a frog can live in water as well as on land

8. Look at the given figure carefully. Identify the organism and the mode of reproduction taking place in it.

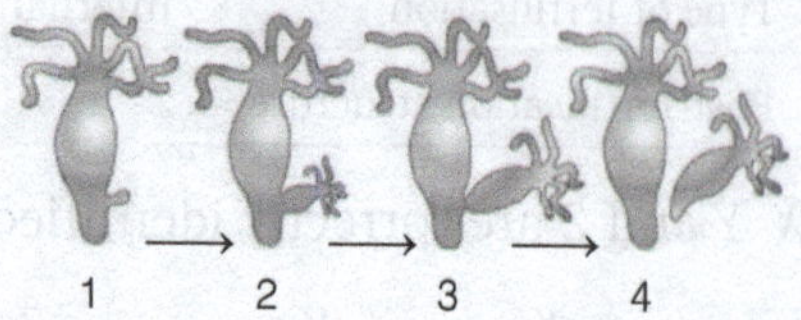

(a) *Planaria*, regeneration
(b) *Hydra*, budding
(c) *Octopus*, regeneration
(d) Yeast, budding

9. The figures given below represent various processes associated with reproduction.
Asexual reproduction is represented by

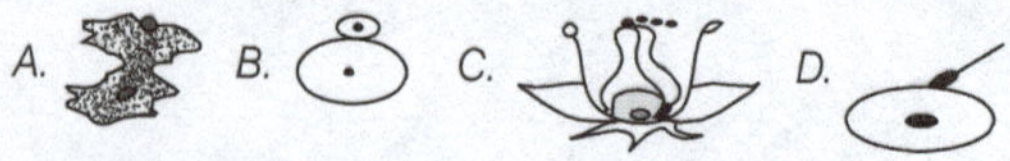

(a) Only *A* (b) Only *B*
(c) *A* and *B* (d) *B* and *D*

10. The figure below shows asexual reproduction in *Amoeba*. Identify the step in which cytokinesis occurs.

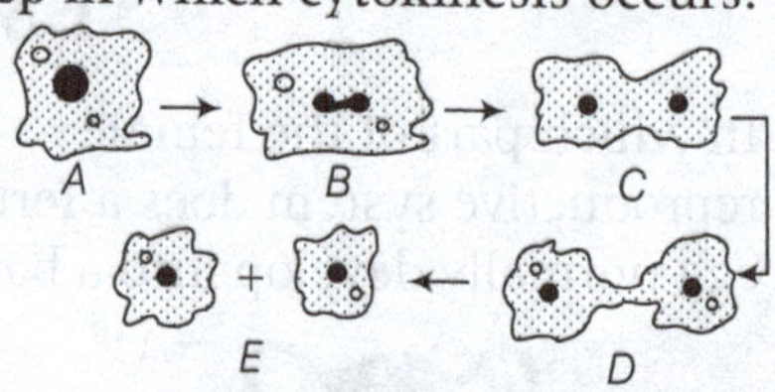

(a) *B* (b) *C* (c) *D* (d) *E*

11. Consider the figures shown below which highlight the part that develops into a new organism by asexual reproduction. An exception to this is

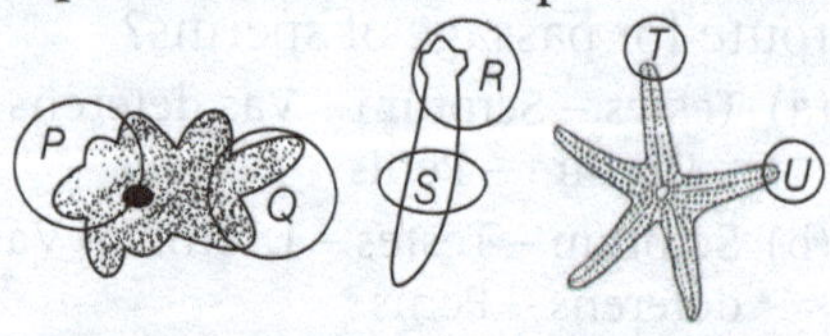

(a) *P*, *Q*, *T* and *U* (b) *R*, *S*, *T* and *U*
(c) *Q*, *R*, *S* and *T* (d) *R*, *T* and *Q*

12. **Assertion** (A) Cloning helps in preserving desirable features of the parent animal for future generation.
Reason (R) Cloning is an asexual method of reproduction.
Which of the following statement is correct?

(a) Both A and R are true and R is the correct explanation of A
(b) Both A and R true, but R is not the correct explanation of A
(c) A is true, but R is false
(d) A is false, but R is true

2 Marks Questions

13. An animal who is known to exhibit-viviparity will show which of the following features.

I. They lay eggs.

II. Eggs are fertilised and developed outside the mother's body always.

III. The sperm meets the ovum inside the mother's body.

IV. All embryos are developed inside the mother's body.

Codes

(a) I, III and IV

(b) I and IV

(c) III and IV

(d) All of the above

14. Which of the following statement(s) is/are incorrect?

I. Human females are oviparous as we given birth to young ones.

II. Usually one egg is fertilised by many sperms.

III. The human embryo develops inside the womb of the mother.

IV. After 9 months of development in the mother's ovary, the baby is ready for delivery.

Codes

(a) Only II

(b) Both I and III

(c) Both II and III

(d) I, II and IV

15. Read the statements given below.

I. IVF is a treatment for infertility when a woman is able to produce ovum however, problems of the Fallopian tube make fertilisation difficult.

II. The animals that give birth to eggs are known as viviparous animals.

III. Unicellular organisms reproducing by binary fission are referred to as 'immortals because actual death of the parent does not occur.

IV. Snakes always exhibit external fertilisation.

Which of the given statements are incorrect?

(a) II, III and IV (b) II and IV

(c) I, II, III and IV (d) I and III

16. Consider the given statements and select the option correctly defining the statement as either True [T] or False [F].

I. Fertilisation is necessary event in asexual reproduction.

II. The new organism produced by asexual reproduction is clone of its parent.

III. An organism, reproducing through sexual reproduction is known as clone.

IV. *Paramecium* is an unicellular organism which reproduce through multiple fission.

V. Animal cloning is done by the transfer of nucleus from a cell to an enucleated cell.

Codes

	I	II	III	IV	V
(a)	T	F	F	F	T
(b)	T	T	F	T	T
(c)	F	T	F	T	T
(d)	F	F	F	T	T

Chapter 07

Reaching the Age of Adolescence

1 Mark Questions

1. Adam's apple is a protrusion of the '*N*' region during the puberty especially marked in the boys. What is *N*?

(a) Muscles (b) Pharynx
(c) Larynx (d) Sebaceous gland

2. Given below are characteristics of a hormone secreted when one reaches puberty.

- It is responsible for breast development.
- It is secreted in girls.

The hormone is

(a) testosterone
(b) oestrogen
(c) growth hormone
(d) Both (a) and (b)

3. Which of the given below options are common in both male and female at puberty?

A. Pubic hair
B. Beard
C. Adam's apple
D. Deep voice
E. Broadening of pelvis
F. Hair under armpits

(a) A, B, D, E, F (b) A, C, E, F
(c) A, F (d) Only F

4. Select the option that defines the correct age at which the rapid growth occurs in male and female

	Male	Female
(a)	12-14 years	10-13 years
(b)	0-3 years	0-12 years
(c)	10-14 years	14 years onwards
(d)	4-12 years	14 years onwards

5. Read the statements given below.

I. The first menstrual flow begins at the puberty.
II. At 45-50 years of age, the menstrual cycle stops.

Which of the following option correctly highlights the terms that describes the events in I and II?

(a) Menopause and menstruation, respectively
(b) Menarche and menstruation, respectively
(c) Menopause and menarche, respectively
(d) Menarche and menopause, respectively

6. Which of the following changes take place during puberty?

A. Milk teeth begin to fall.
B. Children grow taller rapidly.

C. Breasts begin to developed in females.
D. Voice breaks and begins to deepen in males.
E. Hair begins to grow longer.

Codes

(a) A, B and C (b) B, C and D
(c) A, B, C and D (d) A, B, C, D and E

7. Adolescent individuals should be cautious about their diet, because

I. proper diet helps in rapid growth of the body.
II. eating unmonitored diet since adolescents feel hungry all the time results in obesity.

Select the correct option.

(a) I is correct (b) II is correct
(c) Both are correct (d) None are correct

8. A doctor has advised an individual to take regular injection of insulin because of his

(a) high blood pressure
(b) low heat rate
(c) high blood sugar
(d) low metabolic rate

9. *A* is essential for normal functioning of thyroxine hormone secreted by thyroid gland. *A* is identified by which option?

(a) Calcium (b) Sodium
(c) Magnesium (d) Iodine

10. Pick the odd one out.

(a) Calcitonin (b) Testosterone
(c) Adrenaline (d) Trypsin

11. When adrenaline is secreted in large amount, it prepares our body for action. Identify the changes that will not take place in body with the release of this hormone.

(a) Increased heartbeat
(b) Glucose is secreted in urine
(c) Low blood pressure
(d) Rapid breakdown of carbohydrates (glucose)

12. In the figure given below,

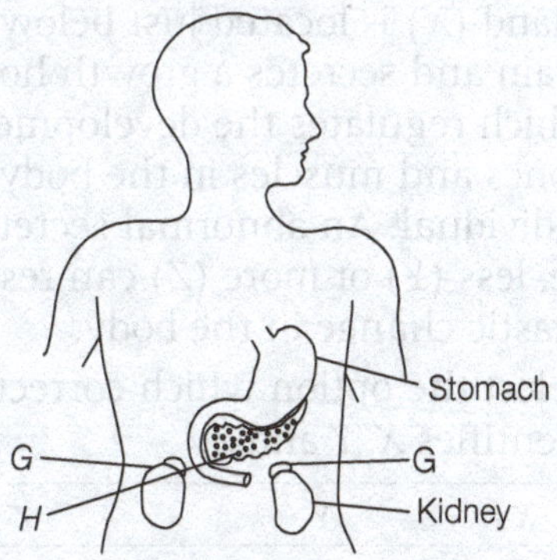

Identify the parts which have following effects on the body.

	Effect on the body
I.	The overall effect is to prepare the body for emergency situations 'fight or flight'. e.g., Running, shouting, etc.
II.	Controls the conversion of excess glucose to glycogen in the liver.

Codes

(a) I—*H* (b) I—*G* and II—*H*
(c) I and II—*G* (d) I and II—*H*

13. Refer to the figure given below where a woman is exhibiting symptoms of a hormone deficiency.

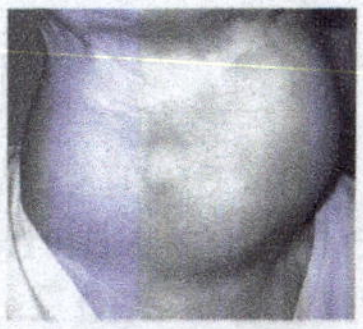

Select the correct statement with respect to the figure.

(a) This condition is associated with a malfunctioning pituitary gland
(b) An insulin injection can temporarily relieve the symptoms of the hormone deficiency
(c) Due to deficiency of thyroxine hormone, causing the gland in neck to enlarge
(d) This occur due to malfunctioning of adrenal gland

2 Marks Questions

14. Gland (X) is located just below the brain and secretes a growth hormone which regulates the development of bones and muscles in the body of an individual. An abnormal secretion, i.e. less (Y) or more (Z) can result in drastic change in the body.

Select the option which correctly identifies X, Y and Z.

	X	Y	Z
(a)	Pituitary	Extremely small body, i.e. Dwarfism	Extremely tall body, i.e. Gigantism
(b)	Hypothalamus	Affects voluntary actions in body	Affects involuntary activities in body
(c)	Thyroid	Weakened body	Strong body
(d)	Adrenal	Heart rate is abnormally slow	Heart rate is abnormally high

15. Study the flowchart given below.

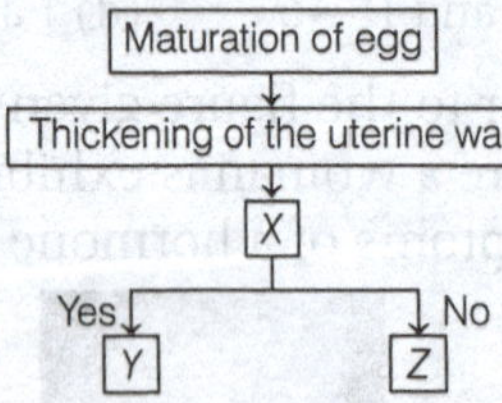

Read the statements given below and select the option which correctly relates with X, Y and Z.

(a) X could be the process of fertilisation where one of the male gametes entering the female reproductive tract fuses with the egg.

(b) For Y-in absence of fertilisation, uterine lining sheds off as menstrual bleeding.

(c) Z-represents establishment of a pregnancy after fusion of gametes.

(d) X-release of eggs from ovaries, Y-fertilisation of gametes and Z-menstruation

16. Read the specification provided below.

I. A acts as an endocrine gland only.
II. B acts as an exocrine gland only.
III. C acts as both the endocrine and exocrine glands.

Identify the glands which can be correctly associated with I, II and III from the box given below.

(i) Sweat gland, (ii) Pancreas, (iii) Prostrate gland, (iv) Pituitary, (v) Salivary gland, (vi) Adrenal gland, (vii) Liver, (viii) Thymus

	I	II	III
(a)	iv, vi and viii	i, iii and v	ii and vii
(b)	i, iii and v	ii and vii	iv, vi and viii
(c)	ii, vi, vii	i, iii and v	iv and viii
(d)	i, iii, v and vii	ii, iv and vi	viii

17. The figure given below shows the female reproductive tract.

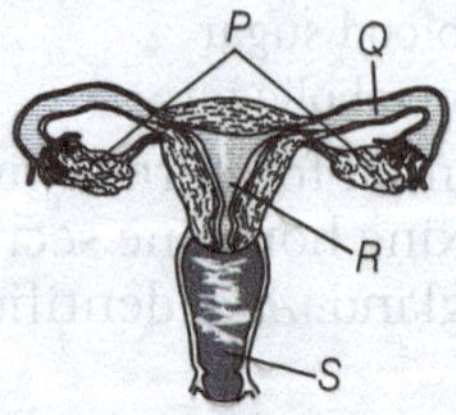

Correlate the given features of the female reproductive tract (I-IV) with their respective parts (P-S).

I. Site of fertilisation.
II. Passage for entry of sperms.
III. Site of gamete production.
IV. Part where development of embryo takes place.

Codes

	I	II	III	IV
(a)	Q	S	P	R
(b)	S	P	R	Q
(c)	P	Q	R	S
(d)	R	S	Q	P

Chapter 08

Force and Pressure

1 Mark Questions

1. Which of the following statement(s) about force is/are false?

I. A force is a push or a pull.
II. A force can stop a moving object.
III. A force can change the direction of a moving object.
IV. A force cannot change the speed of a moving object.

Codes

(a) I and III (b) Only III
(c) II and III (d) Only IV

2. A box was pushed over an equal distance on four different surfaces. The force needed for each surface was recorded on the table below.

Surface	*A*	*B*	*C*	*D*
Force needed	400	575	475	375

On which surface, was the friction least?

(a) *A* (b) *B* (c) *C* (d) *D*

3. Ram and Shyam are shown applying force on a block. If the block moves towards the right which one of the following statements is correct ?

(a) Magnitude of force applied by Ram is greater than that of shyam
(b) Magnitude of force applied by Ram is smaller than that of shyam
(c) Net force on the block is towards Ram
(d) Magnitude of force applied by Ram is equal to that of shyam

4. When the circuit shown in the figure is completed, the hammer strikes the gong.

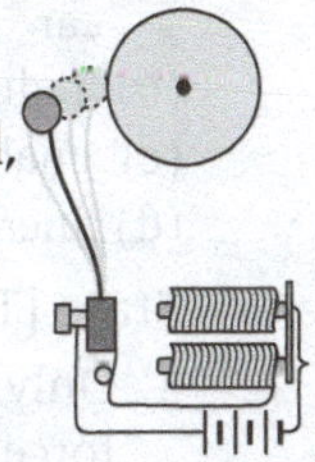

Which of the following force is responsible for the movement of hammer?

(a) Gravitational force
(b) Magnetic force
(c) Electrostatic force
(d) Frictional force

5. Study the diagrams given. How many of these actions involve the use of friction?

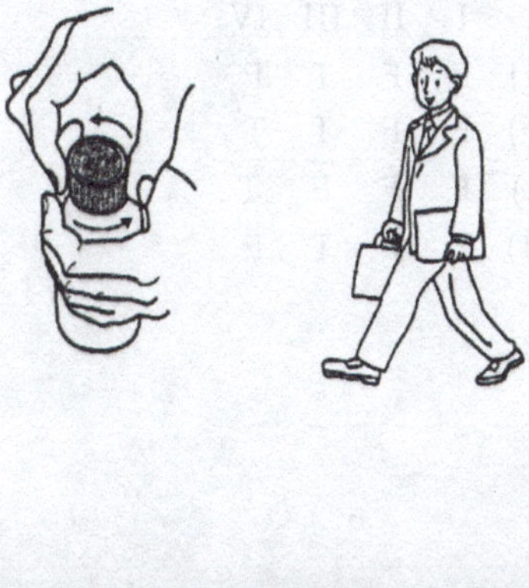

(a) One (b) Two
(c) Three (d) Four

6. The diagram given below shows a rubber tyre.

There are deep treads on the tyre because they ....

(a) increase the stopping distance of the car
(b) reduce the amount of material used
(c) enable the tyre to move smoothly
(d) increase friction

7. State [T] for True and [F] for False.

I. Only the earth exerts gravitational force.
II. Force between two electric charges is called magnetic force.
III. The force per unit area is the pressure on that area.
IV. Muscular force and frictional force are the examples of non-contact forces.

Codes

	I	II	III	IV
(a)	F	F	T	F
(b)	F	F	T	T
(c)	F	F	F	T
(d)	T	F	T	F

8. Study the diagrams given below.

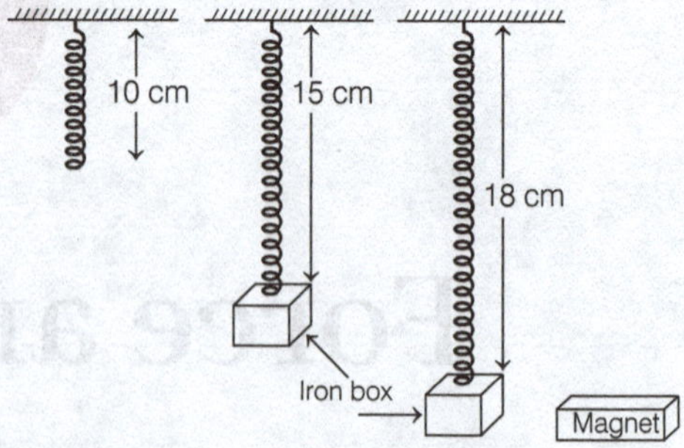

Which type of forces cause the spring to extend in the diagram above?

A. Elastic force exerted by the spring.
B. Magnetic force acting on the iron box.
C. Gravitational force acting on the iron box.
D. Frictional force acting between the iron box and the magnet.

Codes

(a) Only B (b) B and C
(c) A, B and C (d) A, C and D

9. State [T] for True and [F] for False.

I. A force that helps us to walk on road is friction force.
II. Force exerted by one object on another by virtue of their mass is called gravitational force.
III. A force of animals is used to carry out many difficult tasks is called muscular force.
IV. Force between two charged bodies is called magnetic force.

Codes

	I	II	III	IV
(a)	T	T	T	F
(b)	T	T	F	T
(c)	T	T	T	T
(d)	T	F	F	T

10. When two teams pull the rope while playing in a game of tug-of-war, a stage comes when the rope does not move to either side at all. The magnitude of force being applied to the rope by the two teams at that stage will be

(a) greater on first side
(b) greater on second side
(c) equal
(d) sometimes greater on first side than second side

11. Which are the correct metric units for friction and weight?

	Units	
	Friction	**Weight**
(a)	Newton	Kilogram
(b)	Gram-force	Newton
(c)	Newton	Newton
(d)	Joule	Kilogram

12. Figure shows a woman with a parachute. Name the force which is responsible for her downward motion.

(a) Friction force
(b) Force of gravity
(c) Centripital force
(d) Magnetic force

13. We need friction for walking. To put a foot forward, we push the other foot backwards on the ground. The friction between our shoe and the ground acts in the opposite direction and prevents our foot from slipping. Thus, we are able to walk.

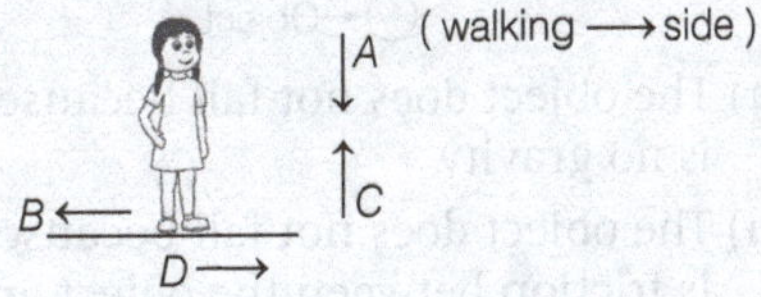

In the above diagram, which arrow represents friction acting between the shoe and the ground?

(a) *A* (b) *B* (c) *C* (d) *D*

14. The figure shows a woman sitting on a chair. The springs in the chair are similar to one another.

Which of the following springs (*A*, *B*, *C* and *D*) has the greatest force acting on it?

(a) *A* (b) *B* (c) *C* (d) *D*

15. The effect of force depends on

A. magnitude of the force applied.
B. area over which force is applied.
C. the direction in which force is applied.
D. All of the above

Codes

(a) A and C (b) B and C
(c) Only D (d) A and B

16. The diagram shows an object hanging from a string. Which of the following is the correct statement about the diagram?

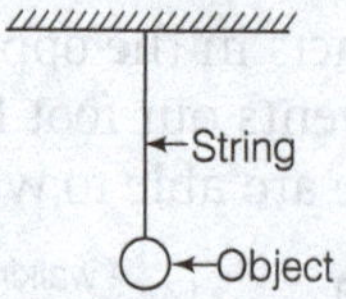

(a) The object does not fall because there is no gravity

(b) The object does not fall because there is friction between the object and the string

(c) The object does not fall because a magnetic force is acting on it

(d) The object does not fall because the string is exerting a force against the Earth's gravity

17. The diagrams below show some ordinary actions. A force is required to carry out each action.

Indicate which of the following is/are correctly matched?

	Action	Force
I.		Pull
II.		Both push and pull
III.		Push
IV.		Push

Codes

(a) Only II (b) II and III

(c) I and IV (d) III and IV

18. Match the statements given in Column I with the suitable words given in Column II and choose the correct answer from the code given below.

Column I	Column II
A. The SI unit of force is	1. Pull
B. Force acts in drawing a bucket of water from a well	2. Newton
C. The force of 1kg-wt acting on an object is equal to	3. 9.8 N
D. Strength of force is expressed in its	4. Magnitude

Codes

	A	B	C	D		A	B	C	D
(a)	1	2	3	4	(b)	2	1	3	4
(c)	4	3	2	1	(d)	2	1	4	3

19. Porters place a round piece of cloth on their heads when they have to carry heavy bags, so that

(a) the bag does not hurt them

(b) it is easier to balance the bags on their heads

(c) the area of contact of the load with their head increases and the pressure decreases

(d) None of the above

20. Which would be least likely to sink into soft ground?

(a) A loaded lorry with four wheels

(b) A loaded lorry with six wheels

(c) An empty lorry with four wheels

(d) An empty lorry with six wheels

21. Geeta take two roads *X* and *Y* of the same weight and equal length have different thickness. They are held vertically on the surface of sand as shown.

Which one of them will sink more?

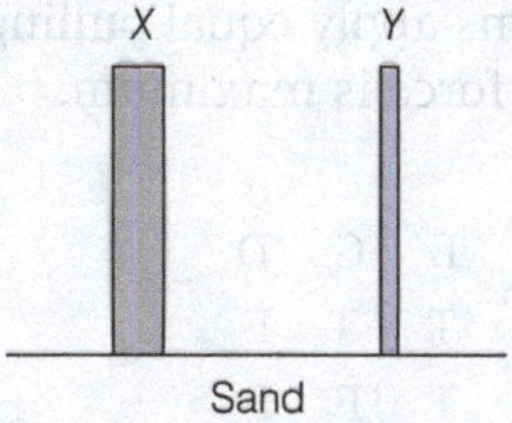

(a) X (b) Y
(c) Both at same time (d) None of these

22. A water tank has four taps fixed at points A, B, C, D as shown in the figure given below. The water will flow out at the same pressure from taps at

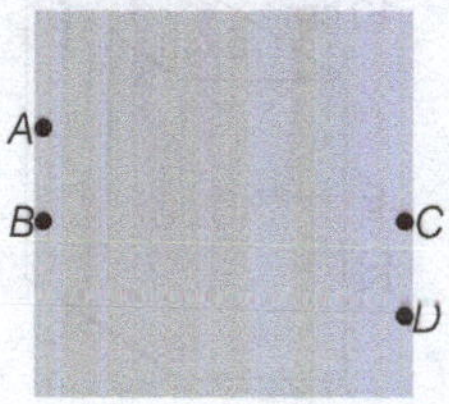

(a) B and C (b) C and D
(c) A and B (d) A and C

23. Sita observe the vessels P, Q, R and S as shown in the figure carefully.

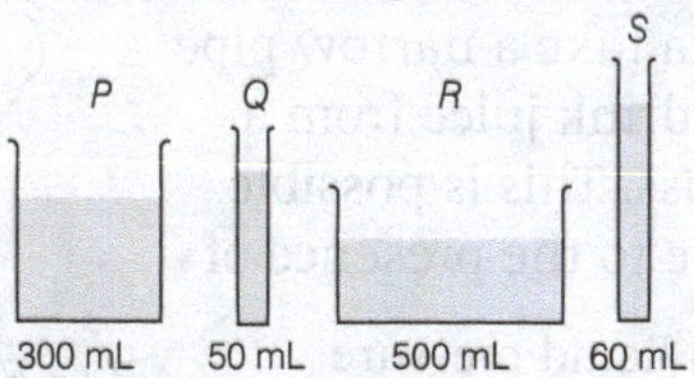

Volume of water taken in each vessel is as shown. Arrange them in order of decreasing pressure at the base of each vessel.

(a) $p_Q > p_P > p_R > p_S$ (b) $p_S > p_Q > p_P > p_R$
(c) $p_S > p_R > p_Q > p_P$ (d) $p_Q > p_S > p_P > p_R$

24.

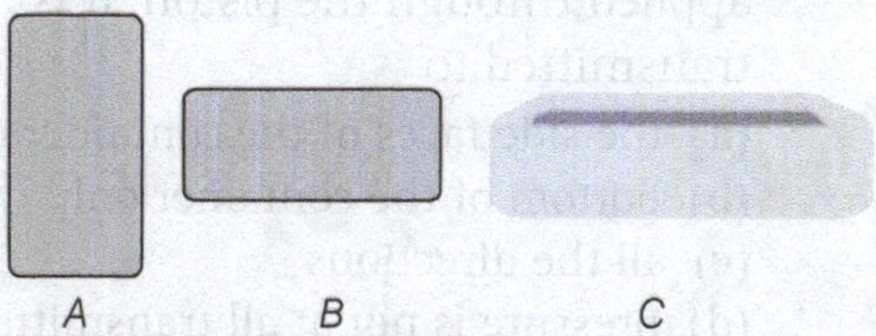

A brick is kept in three different ways on a table as shown in figure. The pressure exerted by the brick on the table will be

(a) maximum in position A
(b) maximum in position B
(c) maximum in position C
(d) equal in all cases

25. Harry says, water exerts pressure on the bottom of the bucket, but Robert says water exerts pressure on the wall of the bucket. Whose statement is correct?

(a) Harry
(b) Robert
(c) Both (a) and (b)
(d) None of the above

26. Given figure shows the cross-section of a dam and its reservoir. The widening of the wall towards the bottom is due to

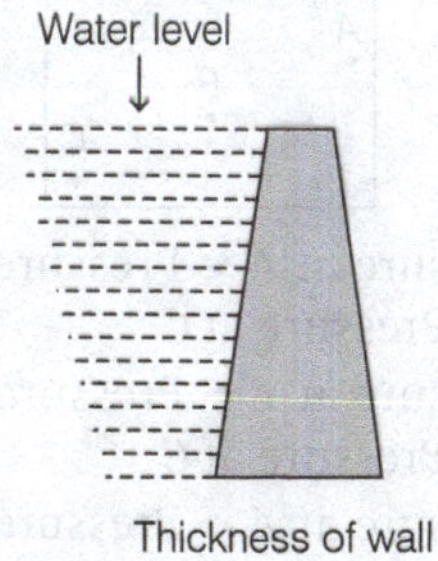

(a) increase in pressure with depth of water
(b) decrease in pressure with depth of water
(c) change in density of water
(d) increase in mass of the wall

27. When we inflate the balloons with air, we find that its size increases. The large number of gas molecules collide with each other and create a large

(a) force (b) pressure
(c) increase in size (d) increase in mass

28. The diagram below shows the vertical sections of a set of vessels, each containing water up to the same height.

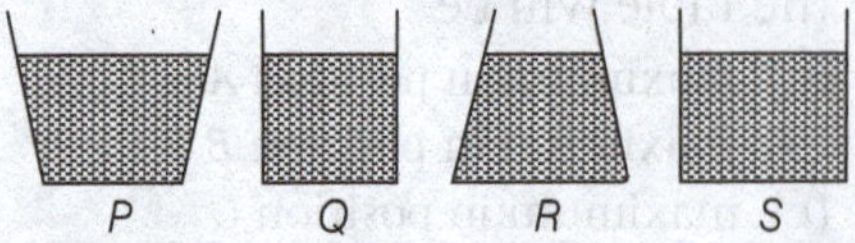

Which of the following statements is correct?

(a) The water exerts the greatest pressure on the base of vessel P

(b) The water exerts greatest pressure on the base of vessel S

(c) The water exerts the same force on the base of each vessel

(d) The water exerts the same pressure on the base of each vessel

29. Figure below shows a container filled with water. Which of the following statement is correct about pressure of water?

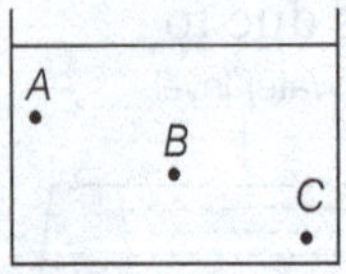

(a) Pressure at $A >$ Pressure at $B >$ Pressure at C

(b) Pressure at $A =$ Pressure at $B =$ Pressure at C

(c) Pressure at $A <$ Pressure at $B >$ Pressure at C

(d) Pressure at $A <$ Pressure at $B <$ Pressure at C

30. State [T] For True and [F] for False.

I. If two forces act in opposite directions, then net force is the difference between the two forces.

II. The nails penetrated into the planks easily because a large force acts on a small area.

III. Water comes out more slowly from an upstair tap than from a similar tap downstairs.

IV. In 'Tug of War', when both the teams apply equal pulling force then net force is maximum.

Codes

	A	B	C	D
(a)	T	T	T	F
(b)	T	T	F	F
(c)	T	F	T	T
(d)	T	F	F	T

31. A brick of weight 80 N stands upright on the ground as shown. What is the pressure, it exerts on the ground?

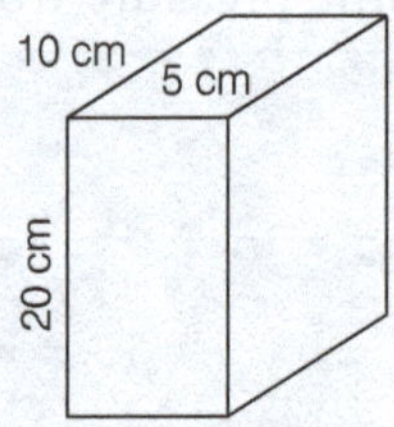

(a) $\frac{80}{20\times 10}$ N/cm^2 (b) $\frac{20\times 10}{80}$ N/cm^2

(c) $\frac{80}{10\times 5}$ N/cm^2 (d) $\frac{10\times 5}{80}$ N/cm^2

32. Sita take a narrow pipe to drink juice from a glass. This is possible due to the presence of

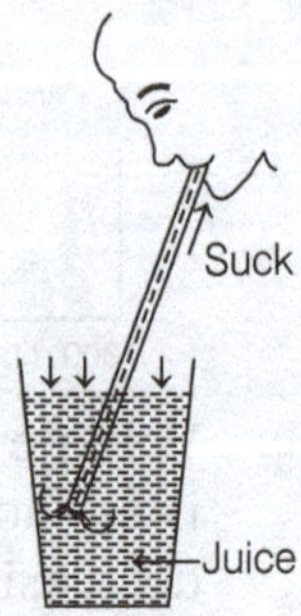

(a) liquid pressure

(b) atmospheric pressure

(c) liquid density

(d) atmospheric density

33. A container containing water is closed from the top using a frictionless piston. When pressure is applied through the piston, it is transmitted to

(a) the side faces of the container only

(b) bottom of the container only

(c) all the directions

(d) pressure is not at all transmitted

34. Which of the following statements is/are incorrect?

I. The ratio of force to area always defines the weight.

II. The envelope of air that surrounds us is known as atmosphere.

III. At a given depth, liquid exerts unequal pressure in all directions.

IV. Liquid exerts pressure only on wall of the container.

Codes

(a) III and IV (b) I and III

(c) I, III and IV (d) II, III and IV

2 Marks Questions

35. When Aryan placed a magnet at the top of the ramp as shown in the figure, the paper clip moved up the ramp and attached to the magnet.

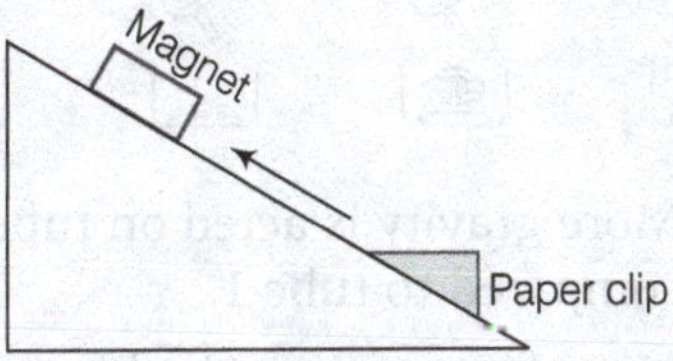

What are the forces acting on the paper clip as it moves along the ramp?

A. Frictional force

B. Magnetic force

C. Elastic potential force

D. Gravitational force

Codes

(a) Only B (b) Both A and D

(c) A, B and D (d) A, B, C and D

36. A boy is pulling a heavy box across the floor as shown below. Which arrows A, B, C and D correctly show the direction of the forces of friction and gravity?

	Friction	Gravity
(a)	*A*	*B*
(b)	*A*	*C*
(c)	*C*	*A*
(d)	*C*	*D*

37. The pictures show some effects of a force.

I. A meteor glowing as it falls through the Earth's atmosphere.	II. A parachutist falling through the air.	III. Brakes slowing down a bicycle.

What is the common factor which is acting in these three situations above?

(a) Friction (b) Gravitational force

(c) Weight (d) Magnetic force

38. Match the Column I with Column II and choose the correct answer from the options given below.

Column I	Column II
A. Contact force	1. Push or pull
B. Pressure	2. Non-contact force
C. Magnitude	3. Muscular force
D. Force	4. Strength of force
E. Force of gravity	5. Force on unit area

Codes

	A	B	C	D	E
(a)	1	2	3	4	5
(b)	3	5	4	1	2
(c)	5	4	3	2	1
(d)	3	4	5	2	1

39. Match the Column I with Column II and choose the correct answer from the codes given below.

Column I	Column II
A. A child running to catch the school bus.	1. Force can make a stationary object to move.
B. A man blowing a balloon.	2. Force can stop a moving object.
C. A woman pushing a table.	3. Force can change the shape of an object.
D. A cricketer catching a ball.	4. Force can make an object move faster.

Codes

	A	B	C	D		A	B	C	D
(a)	4	3	1	2	(b)	3	2	1	4
(c)	1	2	3	4	(d)	2	4	1	3

40. Match the Column I with Column II and choose the correct answer from the codes given below.

Column I	Column II
A. Electrostatic force	1. Attract each other
B. Atmospheric pressure	2. Exert same pressure at equal depth
C. Unlike poles	3. 76 mm of Hg
D. Liquids	4. Force between charges

Codes

	A	B	C	D		A	B	C	D
(a)	1	2	3	4	(b)	4	3	2	1
(c)	4	3	1	2	(d)	1	3	2	4

41. Tom squeezed four identical tubes of toothpaste from the same height above four different plates as shown below. The initial amount of toothpaste in each tube was same.

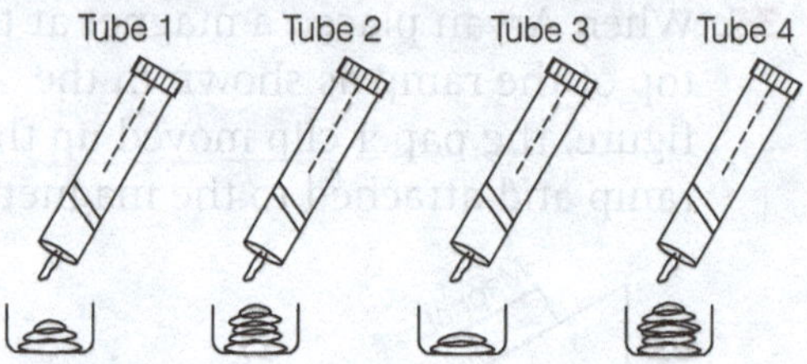

A. More gravity is acted on tube 4 as compared to tube 1.

B. More force was applied on tube 1 as compared to tube 3.

C. There was more toothpaste left in tube 3 compared to tube 2.

Codes

(a) A and B (b) B and C
(c) A and C (d) A, B and C

42. Which of the following statement(s) is/are incorrect?

A. The standard unit of pressure is pascal or Pa.

B. Pressure is area divided by force applied.

C. The bigger the area on which force is applied, the lesser its effect.

D. The knife penetrates easily as the sharp edge has a very small area of contact.

Codes

(a) A and B (b) Only B
(c) B and C (d) A and D

Chapter 09

Friction

1 Mark Questions

1. A man pushes a box across the floor. It slides smoothly but comes to a halt after a while. Which of the given reasons explains why this happen?

(a) Gravity is acting on the box in the direction opposite to the box's movement

(b) Friction is acting on the box in the same direction of the box's movement

(c) Friction is acting on the box in the opposite direction of the box's movement

(d) The heat produced by the box's movement slows down the movement

2. Which arrow shows the direction of the force of friction acting on the runner's shoe?

(a) A (b) B (c) C (d) D

3. An object of weight w is pulled along a rough, horizontal surface by a force P. The force of friction is F.

Which diagram correctly shows the direction of these forces on the object?

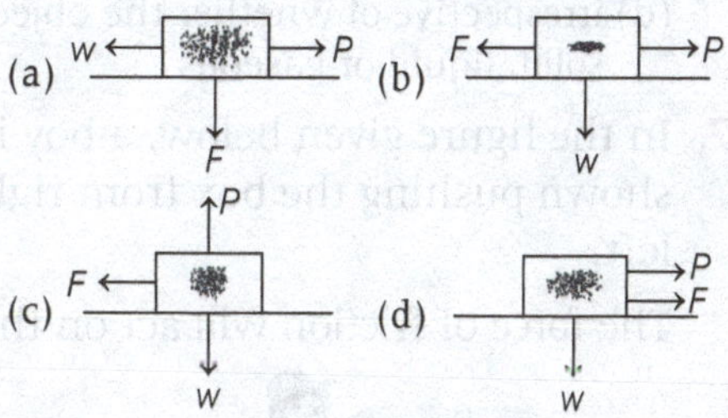

4. Arun carried out an experiment to find out how different surfaces (P, Q, R, S) affect the distance of a car travelling at 60 km/h, which needed to stop once the brakes are applied.

Types of road surface	P	Q	R	S
Stopping distance (m)	20	17	18	15

Which type of road will provide the most friction for the car to stop?

(a) P (b) R

(c) S (d) Q

5. In a large commercial complex, there are four ways to reach the main road. One of the paths has loose soil, the second is laid with polished marble, the third is laid with bricks and the fourth has gravel surface. It is raining heavily and Paheli wishes to reach the main road. The path on which she is least likely to slip is

(a) loose soil (b) polished marble
(c) bricks (d) gravel

6. Whenever the surfaces in contact tend to move or move with respect to each other, the force of friction comes into play

(a) only if the objects are solid
(b) only if one of the two objects is liquid
(c) only if one of the two objects is gaseous
(d) irrespective of whether the objects are solid, liquid or gaseous

7. In the figure given below, a boy is shown pushing the box from right to left.

The force of friction will act on the box

(a) from right to left (←)
(b) from left to right (→)
(c) vertically downwards (↓)
(d) vertically upwards (↑)

8. Ram pushes the box by applying a force of 500 N in horizontal direction, so that the box slides on the floor as shown in figure. Find the point, where the frictional force acting on the box is maximum.

(a) P (b) Q
(c) R (d) P, Q and R

9. When friction is acting in the direction of P, then in which direction do you think the force is applied?

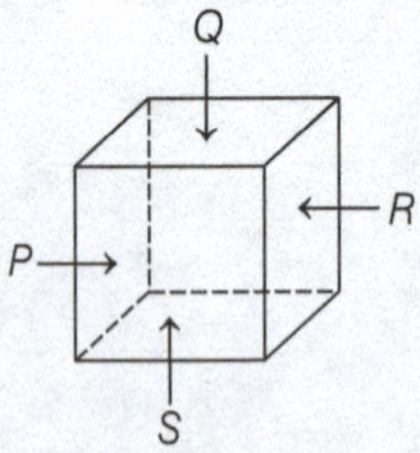

(a) P (b) Q (c) R (d) S

10. Alida runs her toy car on dry marble floor, wet marble floor, newspaper and towel spread on the floor. The force of friction acting on the car on different surfaces in increasing order will be

(a) wet marble floor < dry marble floor < newspaper < towel
(b) newspaper < towel < dry marble floor < wet marble floor
(c) towel < newspaper < dry marble floor < wet marble floor
(d) wet marble floor < dry marble floor < towel < newspaper

11. The diagram given below shows a ball rolling down a slope. The ball comes to a stop by itself. Which of the following statements describes the most likely caused of the ball to stop?

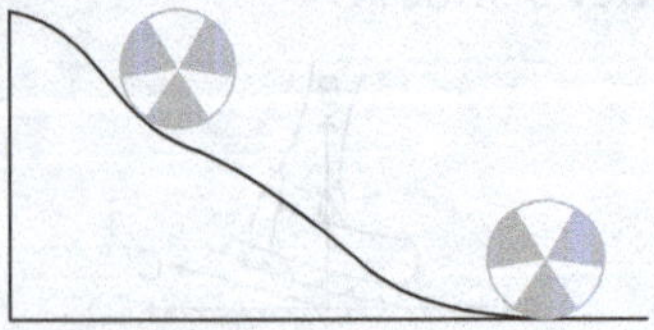

(a) The heat produced as a result of its motion
(b) The speed produced as a result of its motion
(c) The friction between the ball and the surface
(d) The energy produced as a result of its motion

12. A person throws four stones having the same weight on four different surfaces as icy, dry, sandy and cemented. If same force is applied in throwing, then on which surface the stone will cover maximum distance?

(a) Icy surface (b) Dry surface
(c) Sandy surface (d) Cemented surface

13. Door hinge is a jointed device that allows the turning of a door. If we apply oil on door hinges, the friction will

(a) increase
(b) decrease
(c) disappear altogether
(d) will remain unchanged

14. A boy rolls a rubber ball on a wooden surface. The ball travels a short distance before coming to rest. To make the same ball travel longer distance before coming to rest, he may

(a) spread a carpet on the wooden surface
(b) cover the ball with a piece of cloth
(c) sprinkle talcum powder on the wooden surface
(d) sprinkle sand on the wooden surface

15. Four children were asked to arrange forces due to rolling, static and sliding frictions in a decreasing order. Their arrangements are given below. Choose the correct arrangements.

(a) Rolling > static > sliding
(b) Rolling > sliding > static
(c) Static > sliding > rolling
(d) Sliding > static > rolling

16. You must have observed a bull ploughing the field. A bull struggles in its first few steps to pull a plough. Why is it so?

(a) Static friction is greater than sliding friction
(b) Sliding friction is greater than rolling friction
(c) No frictional force acts after the cart is in motion
(d) Air friction is greater during the first few steps of motion

17. A rocket and a bird have a streamlined shaped body (as shown in figure below) because

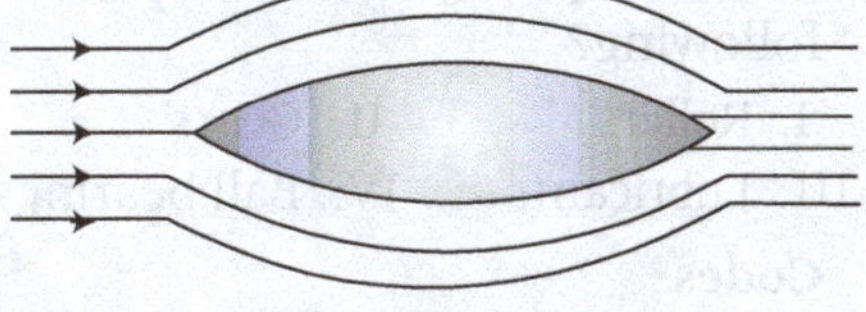

Streamlined body

(a) it gives force to move
(b) it moves through air with minimum friction
(c) it increases the speed of the object
(d) All of the above

18. The bottle in the picture is rolling from P towards S. From which direction should frictional force act to slow down the rolling bottle?

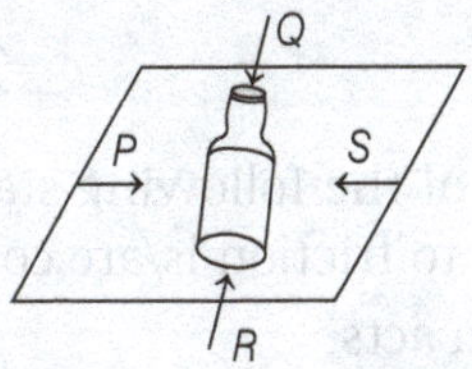

(a) P (b) Q
(c) S (d) R

19. Roller-skating is the travelling on surfaces with roller-skates. It is a form of sport and can also be a form of transportation.
Why do we move faster on roller-skates than on shoes?

(a) The roller-skates have rollers to reduce friction
(b) The roller-skates have more surface in contact with ground
(c) The roller-skates have no gravitational force
(d) The roller-skates absorb heat from the ground

20. We need energy to overcome friction. During friction, unwanted heat energy is produced. Friction can be reduced by the use of which of the following?

I. Rollers II. Gears
III. Lubricants IV. Ball bearings

Codes
(a) I, II and III (b) I, III and IV
(c) II, III and IV (d) I, II and IV

21. When we apply some force on an object held stationary at a place, then force of friction comes into play in direction opposite to the direction of motion of the object.
When the applied force is doubled (object is still at rest), then friction becomes

(a) doubled (b) halved
(c) quadrupled (d) zero

22. Given below is a list of some items/quantities.

I. Lubricants II. Streamlined bodies
III. Heat IV. Polished surface
V. Ball bearing

Pick the odd one(s) out from the above list.
(a) I and IV (b) II and IV
(c) Only III (d) III and V

23. Select the incorrect statement.
(a) Grass and dampness on a cricket ground increase friction
(b) Friction causes parts of a machine to wear out
(c) Moving parts of a car (e.g. wheel) become hot due to friction
(d) Friction is less on a dry floor than a wet floor

24. If the static friction between two surfaces X and Y is found to be 20 N, then the rolling friction between these two surfaces would be
(a) 25 N (b) 50 N (c) 20 N (d) 5 N

2 Marks Questions

25. Which of the following statement(s) related to friction is/are correct?
Friction acts

I. only when an object is in motion.
II. whether an object is moving or not.
III. on a stationary object only.
IV. on an object opposite to the direction of its motion.

Codes
(a) I and IV (b) II and IV
(c) Only III (d) Only II

26. **Statement I** If friction is not present in nature, then life will be easy.
Statement II Without friction, there would be no reaction from ground in a forward direction.

(a) Only statement I is correct.
(b) Only statement II is correct.
(c) Both statements are correct.
(d) Both statements are incorrect.

27. State [T] for True and [F] for False.

I. Friction occurs because most surfaces are not rough.

II. The force of friction is dependent on the weight of body.

III. If an object starts moving, it would never stop if there were no friction.

IV. Friction produces motion.

Codes

	I	II	III	IV
(a)	T	T	F	T
(b)	F	F	T	F
(c)	F	T	T	F
(d)	T	F	F	T

28. Which one of the following statement(s) given below is/are correct?

I. The force of friction depends on the area of the surfaces in contact.

II. Motion opposes friction.

III. It is not possible to cut wood without friction between the saw and wood.

IV. Solids and liquids do not allow things to move in or over them.

Codes

(a) Only I
(b) Only II
(c) Only III
(d) Only IV

29. Which of the following statement(s) given below is/are incorrect?

I. Friction is useful to us in many ways.

II. Meteoroids entering the Earth's atmosphere are burnt up by heat generated from friction with the water.

III. We cannot walk without friction between our feet and the ground.

IV. Rolling friction is greater than static friction.

Codes

(a) I, II and III (b) Only II
(c) I, II and IV (d) II and IV

30. Match the Column I with Column II.

	Column I		Column II
A.	Rough surface	1.	No friction
B.	Wheels	2.	More friction
C.	Streamlined bodies	3.	Less friction
D.	Space	4.	Submarines and rockets

Codes

	A	B	C	D
(a)	2	3	4	1
(b)	1	2	4	3
(c)	3	1	2	4
(d)	2	3	1	4

Chapter 10

Sound

1 Mark Questions

1. When a whistle is blown, it produces sound. Which part of whistle vibrates to produce sound?

(a) Body of whistle
(b) Mouth of the person
(c) Air
(d) All of the above

2. Naveen arranged seven similar glasses with water on the table. Each glass had different levels of water. He played different tunes on it using two sticks to tap the water filled glasses. What has he made?

(a) Harmonica (b) Sarangi
(c) Jal tarang (d) Ghatak

3. A student performs the following activity as shown in the figure below.

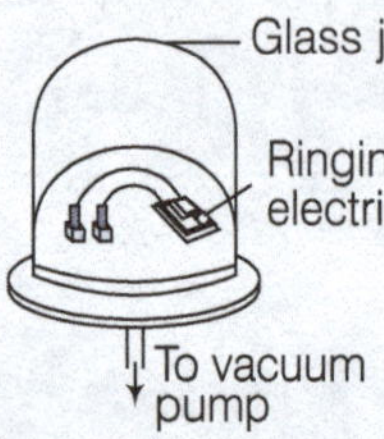

What do you think happened as air was pumped out of the jar and he rang the bell?

(a) The sound became louder
(b) The sound became fainter first and louder once all the air was pumped out
(c) The sound could not be heard anymore
(d) The sound was the same as before

4. A list of medium is given as below.

I. Wood
II. Water
III. Air
IV. Vacuum

In which of these media can sound travel?

(a) I and II (b) I, II and III
(c) III and IV (d) II, III and IV

5. Sound travels with different speed in different medium. The speed of sound is different due to the fact that, different medium has different density given below some objects are written.

1. Air 2. Water
3. Wood 4. Steel

Which among the following object, is a best medium in which the sound will travel fastest ?

(a) Only 4 (b) Only 1 and 2
(c) 1, 2 and 3 (d) Only 1

6. Take four jars with different amount of water. Hit the rim of the jars with the pencil. In which one of the following cases, the intensity of sound will be maximum?

(a) The jar filled completely
(b) Jar half-filled
(c) Jar filled less than half
(d) Jar filled more than half

7. Given figure represents production of sound by glasses filled with water by different amount. When a boy hit the rim of the glasses with pencil, which of them produces sound of maximum intensity?

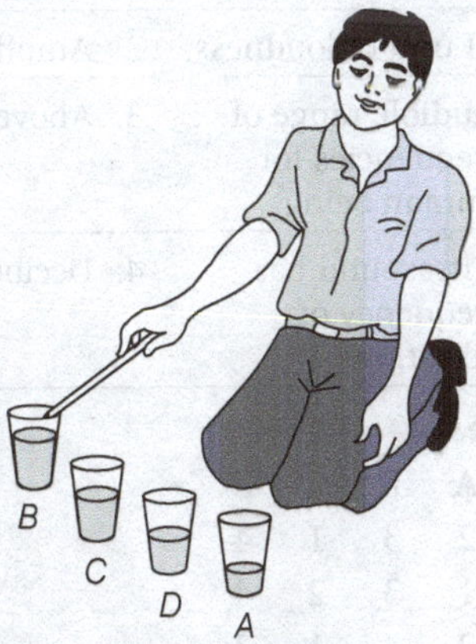

(a) *A* (b) *B* (c) *C* (d) *D*

8. Which of the following is true about the speed of sound through solids?

	Solid	Liquid	Gas
(a)	Slowest	Fastest	Fastest
(b)	Average speed	Fastest	Slowest
(c)	Slowest	Fastest	Average speed
(d)	Fastest	Slowest	Slowest

9. Which of the following does not produce a sound wave?

I. A bell ringing in a glass jar with all the air pumped out.
II. A gun fired in a room with no echoes.
III. A hammer hitting a block of rubber.
IV. An explosion in outer space.

Codes

(a) I, II and III (b) II, III and IV
(c) Only IV (d) I and IV

10. What is the correct order(slowest → fastest) for the speed of sound in air, steel and water?

(a) Air < steel < water
(b) Air < water < steel
(c) Water < air < steel
(d) Water < steel < air

11. A person tries to hear an approaching train by pressing his ear on the track. He will be able to hear because

(a) sound travels faster in solids
(b) sound travels faster in air
(c) railway track starts vibrating
(d) None of the above

12. The names of musical instruments are given as below.

I. Guitar II. Sitar III. Tabla
IV. Violin V. Piano

Pick the odd ones out from the above instruments.

(a) I and II (b) III and IV
(c) III and V (d) IV and V

13. Which of the following is/are incorrect about the production and propagation of sound?

I. Sound is produced by vibrations.
II. Sound requires a medium for propagation.

III. Light and sound both require a medium for propagation.

IV. Sound travels slower than light.

Codes

(a) I and IV (b) I, III and IV
(c) Only III (d) III and IV

14. Which of the following statements is/are incorrect ?

I. Sound is produced by vibrations.

II. Sound can be hear in vaccum.

III. Sound requires a medium for propagation.

IV. Sound speed is slow than speed of light.

Codes

(a) I, II, III and IV (b) Only III
(c) Only II (d) Only IV

15. Which of the following statements is/are correct?

I. Sound can propagate through air.

II. Sound can't propagate through water.

III. Sound can propagate through metal.

Choose the correct option .

(a) Only I (b) Both I and II
(c) I, II and III (d) Both I and III

16. Which of the following statements is/are correct about oscillatory motion of a particle?

(a) Oscillatory motion is periodic
(b) Oscillatory motion has fixed time period
(c) Non-oscillatory motion does not have constant time period
(d) All of the above

17. Human ear is a very sensitive device that has various parts which performs different functions to transmit sound from surroundings to the brain. Which part of the ear does not vibrate while detecting sound?

(a) Eardrum (b) Anvil
(c) Stirrup (d) Eustachian tube

18. Which of the following is not a use of ultrasound?

I. Sonography to check development of unborn babies.

II. Ultrasound for cleaning tartar from teeth.

III. Ultrasound for echolocation to determine depth of ocean.

IV. Ultrasound treatment of tumours in patients suffering from cancer.

Codes

(a) I and III (b) Only II
(c) Only III (d) II, III and IV

19. Match the Column I with Column II.

Column I	Column II
A. Loudness of sound.	1. 20 Hz to 20000 Hz
B. SI unit of loudness.	2. Amplitude
C. Audible range of frequencies for human beings.	3. Above 20000 Hz
D. Ultrasound has frequency of vibrations.	4. Decibel

Codes

	A	B	C	D
(a)	2	3	1	4
(b)	1	3	2	4
(c)	2	4	1	3
(d)	3	2	1	4

20. Four different whistles when blown, emit pure notes with the frequencies shown.

0.1 kHz, 1 kHz, 10 kHz, 100 kHz

How many of the frequencies are above the normal audible range for humans?

(a) 1 (b) 2 (c) 3 (d) 4

21. The sound from the surrounding entering into our ear is collected by pinna. The sound which enters into our ear is not of high amplitude. They are amplified inside our ear. The part of the ear which does this work is
(a) eardrum
(b) hammer, anvil and stirrup
(c) ear canal
(d) cochlea

22. Some animals like elephants, whales and rhinoceroses can produce infrasonic waves. Which of the following is infrasonic sound?
(a) 15 Hz (b) 150 Hz
(c) 1500 Hz (d) 15000 Hz

23. Fill in the blanks and choose the correct option.
I. The voice of a female is different from a male. It is due to .... of sound.
II. The sounds of too low frequency which can not be heard by human is called ....
III. When the amplitude of vibration is large. The sound produced is ....
IV. Sound can travel through ....

Codes

	I	II	III	IV
(a)	pitch	infrasonic	loud	vaccum
(b)	pitch	ultrasonic	loud	vaccum
(c)	pitch	infrasonic	loud	water
(d)	loud	infrasonic	pitch	water

24. Sonic vibrations were sent down from a ship return after 20 s. What is the depth of the sea if the speed of sound in water is 1.5 kms^{-1}?
(a) 150 m
(b) 3 km
(c) 15 km
(d) 750 m

25. Choose a correct option from the following matrix.

	Pitch	Loudness	Noise	Music
(a)	Amplitude	Frequency	Irregular vibration	Regular vibration
(b)	Frequency	Amplitude	Regular vibration	Irregular vibration
(c)	Frequency	Amplitude	Irregular vibration	Regular vibration
(d)	Amplitude	Frequency	Regular vibration	Irregular vibration

26. Find the True [T] and False [F] statements and choose the correct option from the codes given below.
I. The highest audible range of frequency for human ears is 20000 Hz.
II. Light and sound both require a medium for propagation.
III. Sound waves travel faster in air than in water.
IV. Higher the amplitude of vibration, lesser is the pitch.

Codes

	I	II	III	IV
(a)	T	T	F	F
(b)	F	T	F	T
(c)	T	F	T	F
(d)	T	F	F	F

27. Bees which are not carrying honey, fly with a flapping frequency of 440 Hz while those which are carrying honey, fly with a flapping frequency of 300 Hz. The sound made by bees which are not carrying honey has
(a) a long pitch
(b) a higher pitch
(c) a smaller loudness
(d) a greater loudness

28. Look at the given images of an oscilloscope. Image I represents reference sound.

Identify the correct statement.

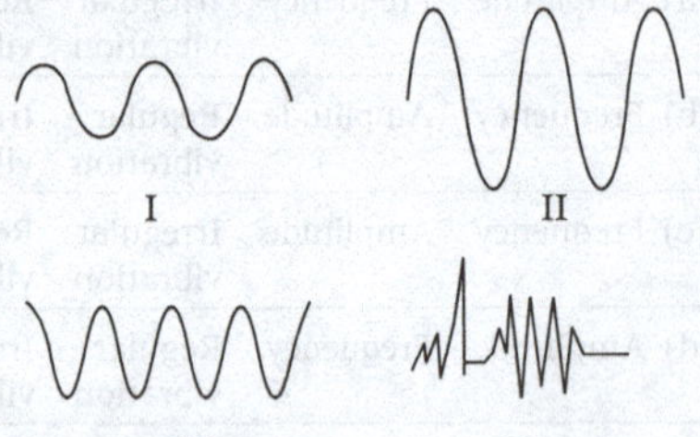

(a) Image II represents a higher frequency than III
(b) Image III represents a louder sound than I
(c) Image III represents a higher frequency than I
(d) Image IV represents a louder sound than I

29. A list of various characteristics of sound is given as below.

I. Shrillness II. Pitch
III. Frequency IV. Loudness
V. Speed

Pick the odd ones out from the above characteristics.

(a) I and III (b) I and IV
(c) IV and V (d) II and V

30. Lightening can be seen, the moment it occurs. Seema observes lightening in her area. She hears the sounds 10 s later she observed lightening. How far is she from the place where lightening occurs?

(Speed of sound = 330 m/s)

(a) 300 m (b) 2800 m
(c) 3300 m (d) 2900 m

31. Lightening can be seen the moment it occurs. Paheli observes lightning in her area. She hears the sound 5s after she observed lightening. How far is she from the place where lightning occurs?

(Speed of sound = 330 m/s)

(a) 16.5 km (b) 1.65 km
(c) 165 km (d) 3.35 km

32. A pendulum makes 40 oscillations in 20 s. The frequency of these oscillation comes out to be.

(a) 2 Hz (b) 4 Hz
(c) 60 Hz (d) 800 Hz

33. The sound from a mosquito is produced when it vibrates its wings at an average rate of 500 vibrations. What is the time period of vibration?

(a) 2 s (b) 0.2 s
(c) 0.02 s (d) 0.002 s

34. A child plays a note on a trumpet. She then plays a louder note of higher pitch. How do the amplitude and frequency of the second sound compare with the first?

	Amplitude of second sound	**Frequency of second sound**
(a)	Larger	Larger
(b)	Larger	Smaller
(c)	Smaller	Larger
(d)	Smaller	Smaller

35. Read the following statements and choose the correct answer from the codes given below.

Statement I All noisy operations must be combusted away from any residential area.

Statement II TV and music system in the house should be run at low volumes to reduce noise pollution.

(a) Only I statement is correct.
(b) Only II statement is correct.
(c) Both I and II are correct.
(d) Both I and II are incorrect.

2 Marks Questions

36. Ram take a stick and stuck against drum in vaccum.

Given below some observations are given in the form of statements.

I. The drum will vibrate.

II. The drum will not vibrate.

III. Ram can able to hear the sound of vibrations.

IV. Ram can not hear the sound of vibrations.

Codes

(a) I and III (b) I and IV

(c) II and IV (d) II and III

37. Find the True [T] and False [F] statements and choose the correct option from the codes given below.

I. A tuning fork, a guitar string and the skin of a drum produce sound because they are in the state of vibration.

II. Light requires a medium to travel but sound can travel in vacuum.

III. Sound propagates in parallel directions only.

IV. The drum and tabla are percussion instruments.

Codes

	I	II	III	IV		I	II	III	IV
(a)	T	F	T	F	(b)	T	T	T	F
(c)	F	T	F	T	(d)	T	F	F	T

38. Which of the following statement(s) is/are correct?

I. The lower limit of frequency that can be heard by the average human ear is 20 Hz.

II. Sound higher than 20000 Hz is called infrasonic.

III. Auditory nerve carries the signals from inner ear to the brain.

IV. Infrasonic waves are used to measure the depth of a sea.

Codes

(a) Only I

(b) I and III

(c) III and IV

(d) All of the above

39. Three different vibrating objects produce three types of sounds *X*, *Y* and *Z*. The sounds *X* and *Y* cannot be heard by a man having normal range of hearing but sound *Z* can be heard easily. The sound *X* can be heard by a bat whereas sound *Y* can be heard by a rhinoceros. What types of sounds are *X*, *Y* and *Z*?

Codes

	X	*Y*	*Z*
(a)	audible	ultrasonic	infrasonic
(b)	infrasonic	ultrasonic	audible
(c)	ultrasonic	infrasonic	audible
(d)	audible	infrasonic	ultrasonic

40. Which of the following statement(s) is/are incorrect about noise?

I. Vehicles should have proper silencers.

II. Sudden exposure to high noise can cause a heart attack.

III. Use of amplifiers and loudspeakers should not be restricted.

IV. Planting of trees helps reduce noise.

Codes

(a) I, II and III

(b) II and III

(c) Only II

(d) I and IV

41. Match the Column I with Column II.

Column I	Column II
A. Oscillation	1. Maximum displacement of a wave.
B. Amplitude	2. Distance between two consecutive peaks.
C. Frequency	3. To and for motion of wave.
D. Wavelength	4. Number of oscillations of sound wave.

Codes

	A	B	C	D
(a)	3	1	4	2
(b)	3	2	4	1
(c)	4	1	3	3
(d)	4	2	1	3

42. State [T] for True and [F] for False.

I. Infrasonic waves are used to kill bacteria in liquids.

II. Ultrasonic waves are produced by the vibration of the Earth's surface during the earthquake.

III. Noise pollution may cause partial hearing impairment.

IV. The sound having frequency less than 20 Hz are called infrasound.

Codes

	I	II	III	IV		I	II	III	IV
(a)	T	T	F	F	(b)	F	T	T	F
(c)	T	F	F	T	(d)	F	F	T	T

43. Given below a figure of ear is shown. Which part of the ear is used to amplify the sound?

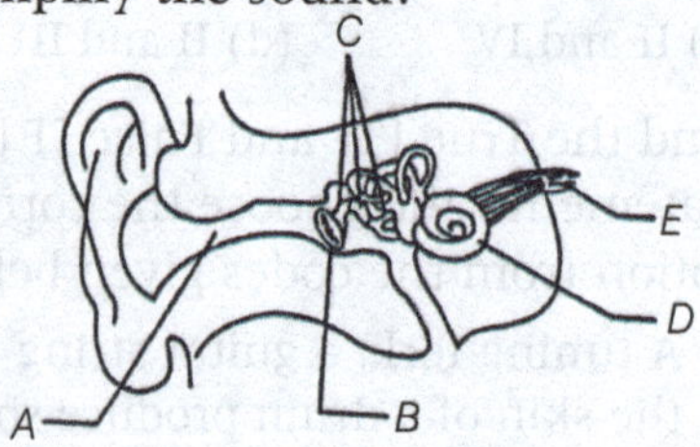

(a) *A* (b) *B*

(c) *D* and *E* (d) *C*

Chapter 11

Chemical Effects of Electric Current

1 Mark Questions

1. When current is passed through molten sodium chloride, then

(a) sodium is deposited at the positive electrode and chlorine gas is formed at the negative electrode

(b) sodium is evaporated and chloride ions are formed at the negative electrode

(c) sodium is deposited at the positive electrode and chlorine is deposited at the negative electrode

(d) sodium is deposited at the negative electrode and the chlorine is deposited at the positive electrode

2. Complete the following reaction with the given options.

$CuSO_4 \xrightarrow{\text{Current}}$ ____ + ____

(a) S^{2-}, O_2^- (b) Cu^{2+}, SO_4^{2-}
(c) Cu^{2+}, O_2^- (d) Cu^{2+}, O_2

3. A box of items is given as below.

I. Milk
II. Impure water
III. Honey
IV. Glass

Which of these conduct electricity?

(a) I and III (b) Only II
(c) II and III (d) Only IV

4. A scientist needed a liquid conductor for his experiment. He found that he had only pure water. What should he do to make it a conductor?

(a) Heat it to 100°C (b) Add sugar to it
(c) Add salt to it (d) None of these

5. In an electrochemical cell, the two electrodes connected with battery are dipped into electrolyte. The electrode connected to positive terminal of a battery is

(a) anode (b) pole
(c) cathode (d) photodiode

6. Which of the following is a device used to determine whether a substance is a good or poor conductor of electricity?

(a) Electric tester (b) Conduction tester
(c) Cathode ray (d) Spark plug

7. Which of the following statement(s) is/are incorrect?

A. Conductors have more free charge on the surface than insulators.
B. Conductors allow charge to flow through them more easily than insulators.
C. Non-metals are good conductors.

D. Electric wires are usually covered by insulators.

Codes

(a) A and B (b) B and C
(c) Only C (d) Only D

8. In the given figure, glowing of bulb shows that

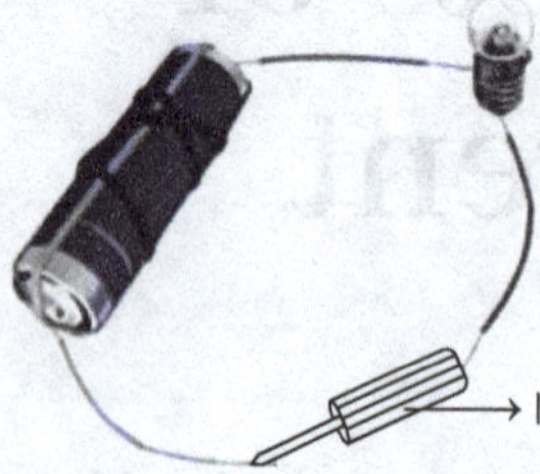

(a) circuit is complete
(b) iron is a good conductor
(c) iron is an insulator
(d) Both (a) and (b)

9. An electric current is defined as the flow of charge through a conductor. An electric current can produce

(a) heating effect (b) chemical effect
(c) magnetic effect (d) All of these

10. When electric current is passed through a conducting solution, there is a change of colour of the solution. This indicates

(a) the chemical effect of current
(b) the heating effect of current
(c) the magnetic effect of current
(d) the lightening effect of current

11. Like solids, some liquids also conduct electricity. Such liquids are called electrolytes. An electrolyte

(a) has positive charge
(b) has negative charge
(c) should be able to conduct charge without dissociating
(d) should be able to form positive and negative ions

12. Given figure represents the electrolysis of water. To which carbon rod, hydrogen (H^+) ion will be attracted?

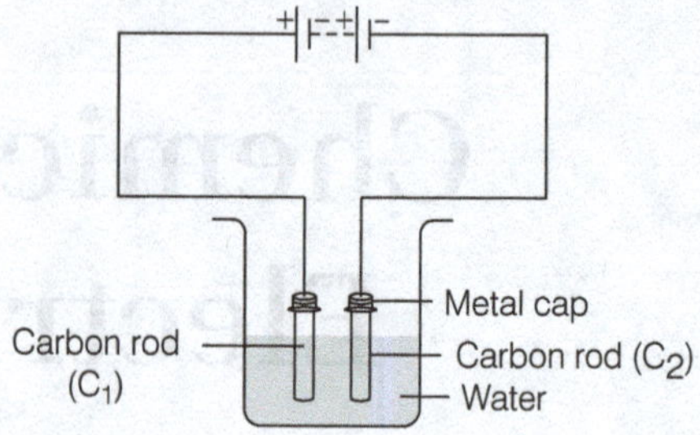

(a) C_1
(b) C_2
(c) On both C_1 and C_2
(d) Will remain in solution

13. A box of liquids is given as below.

I. Lemon juice
II. Sugar solution
III. Dilute hydrochloric acid
IV. Distilled water

Which of the following liquids does not conduct electricity?

(a) I, II and IV
(b) Only III
(c) III and IV
(d) II and IV

14. In a metallic wire, the free electrons are responsible for the flow of electric current. When the ends of metallic wire are not connected to a battery, then

(a) electrons move from positive electrode to negative electrode
(b) electrons move from negative electrode to positive electrode
(c) electrons move in random directions
(d) protons move in random direction in such a way that their net movement in a unit volume is zero

15. See the given figure,
The greenish-blue spot is formed around positive electrode inserted in the surface of a cut potato. which one of the following is correct observation ?

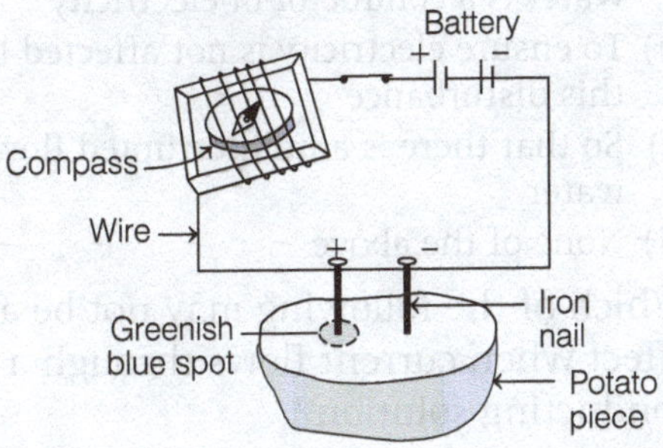

(a) More electrons are produced which move from negative to positive terminal
(b) Less electrons are produced which move from positive to negative terminal
(c) More electrons are produced which move positive to negative terminal
(d) The potato have rotted there

16. Electroplating is one of the main uses of electrolysis. A metal is released in the electrolysis of a salt. It gets deposited on the
(a) anode
(b) cathode
(c) half on anode, half on cathode
(d) side of the container

17. The bulb does not glow in the set up shown in figure below. Which of the following reasons is/are correct ?

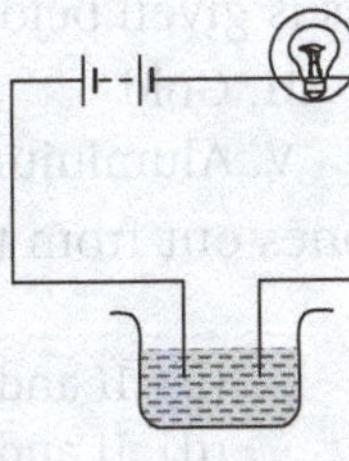

I. The current is not produced by the given liquid and hence, bulb not glow.
II. Connections are loose
III. Bulb is fused
IV. Cell are used up

Codes

(a) I, II and III (b) Only III
(c) II and IV (d) All of these

18. Which of the following solution will not make the bulb in the diagram glow?

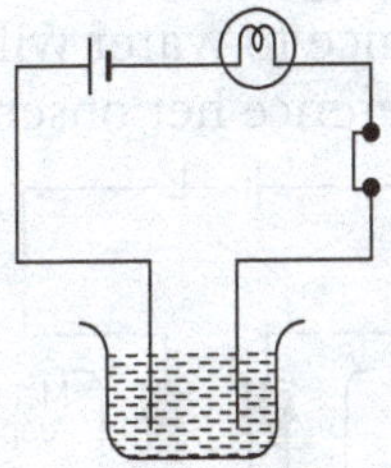

(a) Sodium chloride
(b) Copper sulphate
(c) Silver nitrate
(d) Sugar solution in diluted water

19. Name the liquid which when tested in the manner shown in figure below may cause the magnetic needle to deflect.

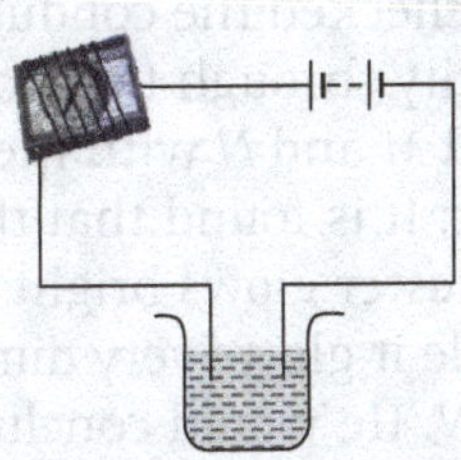

(a) Sugar solution (b) Distilled water
(c) Honey (d) Tap water

20. Arun went to the seaside. He collected some seawater for testing. He tested some drinking water and also the seawater with his tester. He finds that his tester needle deflects more in case of seawater. Why?

(a) Because, drinking water is a poor conductor
(b) Because, seawater is a poor conductor
(c) Because, seawater is an insulator
(d) Because, seawater is very salty and salt solution is a good conductor of electricity

21. Neena made the circuit as shown in figure. She wanted to observe what happens when an electric current is passed through water. But she forgot to add a few drops of lemon juice to water will it make any difference her observations?

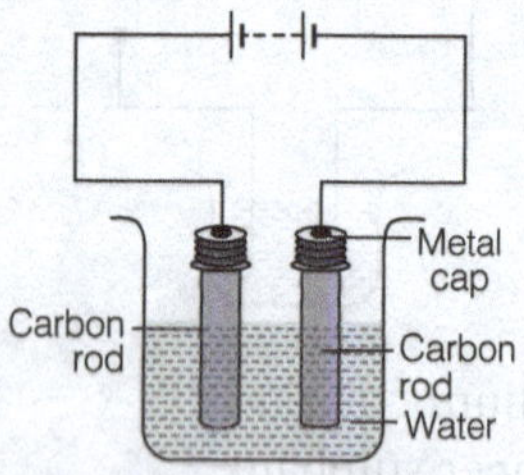

(a) Will increase the conductivity of solution
(b) Will decrease the conductivity of solution
(c) No difference in conductivity
(d) None of the above

22. Rahul checked the conduction of electricity through two liquids labelled *M* and *N* with the help of a tester. It is found that the bulb of the tester glows bright for liquid *M*, while it glows very dimly for liquid *N*. He would conclude that
(a) liquid *M* is a better conductor than liquid *N*
(b) liquid *N* is a better conductor than liquid *M*
(c) both liquids are equally conducting
(d) conducting properties of liquid cannot be compared in this manner

23. In case of a fire, before the fireman uses the water hoses to throw water to douse fire they shut off the electricity supply of the area. Why?
(a) To prevent electrocution because ordinary water is a conductor of electricity
(b) To ensure electricity is not affected by this disturbance
(c) So that there is a uninterrupted flow of water
(d) None of the above

24. Which of the following may not be an effect when current flows through a conducting solution?
I. Change of colour of solution
II. Bubbles of gases
III. Deposits of metal on electrodes

Codes
(a) Only I (b) Only II
(c) Only III (d) None of these

25. Select the correct statement.
(a) LED consumes much lower electricity, so they are economical
(b) They find applications for few purposes
(c) Ordinary bulb can glow whether the current supply is high or low
(d) LEDs are available only in yellow colour

26. In case of LED, there are two terminals. Which of the following matching is correct?
(a) Longer terminal — Positive terminal
(b) Shorter terminal — Positive terminal
(c) Longer terminal — Negative terminal
(d) None of the above

27. A list of metals is given below.
I. Silver II. Gold III. Sodium
IV. Chromium V. Aluminium
Pick the odd ones out from the given metals.
(a) I and III (b) II and IV
(c) III and V (d) II and V

28. Which of the following statements is/are correct?

I. There is always a chemical change when electricity is passed through any liquid.

II. Electroplating means deposition of a layer of desired metal over other without electricity.

III. Tins cans used for storing food are made by electroplating tin over iron.

IV. Chromium does not have shiny appearance. It gets corrode.

Codes

(a) Only III
(b) I and III
(c) Only I
(d) I, II and IV

29. Select the incorrect statement.

(a) We can use a magnetic compass in a circuit of a conduction tester
(b) We can use a LED in the circuit of a conduction tester
(c) We can use a torch bulb or LED in the circuit of a conduction tester
(d) We can use iron filings in the circuit of a conduction tester

30. Boojho's uncle has set up an electroplating factory near his village. He should dispose off the waste of the factory

(a) in the nearby river
(b) in the nearby pond
(c) in the nearby cornfield
(d) according to the disposal guidelines of the local authority

31. Which of the following statements is/are incorrect?

I. The closed path through which the current flows is called circuit.

II. Most of the conducting liquids are the solutions of acids, bases and salts.

III. When electric current is passed through copper sulphate solution, copper gets deposited on the plate connected to the negative terminal of the battery.

IV. LED glows when a large electric current passes through it.

Codes

(a) I, II and III (b) II and IV
(c) Only IV (d) II, III and IV

2 Marks Questions

32. Match the Column I with Column II and choose the correct answer from the codes given below.

Column I		Column II	
A.	CFLs	1.	Cost efficient
B.	LEDs	2.	Non-conducting
C.	Closed path	3.	Contain toxic mercury
D.	Milk	4.	Electric circuit

Codes

	A	B	C	D		A	B	C	D
(a)	2	1	4	3	(b)	3	1	4	2
(c)	1	2	4	3	(d)	2	1	3	4

33. State [T] for True and [F] for False.

I. The passage of an electric current through a conducting liquid cases chemical reactions.

II. During electroplating, the object to be electroplated is made anode.

III. The chemical effect of electric current is used in purification of salts.

IV. The chemical reaction brought about by an electric current may produce changes in the colour of solutions.

Codes

	I	II	III	IV
(a)	F	T	T	F
(b)	T	F	F	T
(c)	T	T	F	F
(d)	T	T	T	F

34. State [T] for True and [F] for False.

I. Most liquids that are good conductors are solution of acids, bases and salts.

II. All wires used in electric circuits should be covered with conducting material.

III. Magnetic effect of current is responsible for the glow of the bulb in an electric circuit.

IV. Adding common salt to distilled water makes it good conductor.

V. Cathode is positive electrode.

Codes

	I	II	III	IV	V
(a)	F	T	F	T	T
(b)	T	F	F	T	F
(c)	T	T	T	F	F
(d)	F	F	F	T	T

35. State (T) for True and (F) for False.

I. Adding of sugar makes the pure water conducting.

II. During the electrolysis of water, hydrogen gas is liberated at the anode.

III. Electrolysis is a chemical change.

IV. Some liquids are good conductors of electricity and some are poor conductors.

Codes

	I	II	III	IV		I	II	III	IV
(a)	F	F	F	T	(b)	F	T	F	T
(c)	T	F	T	F	(d)	F	F	T	T

36. Match the Column I with Column II and choose the correct answer from the codes given below.

	Column I		Column II
A.	Insulator	1.	Citric acid
B.	Conductor	2.	Poor conductor
C.	Electrolyte in lemon juice	3.	Distilled water
D.	Non-metal	4.	Sea water

Codes

	A	B	C	D
(a)	4	3	1	2
(b)	4	3	2	1
(c)	3	4	1	2
(d)	3	4	2	1

37. Match the Column I with Column II and choose the correct answer from the codes given below.

Column I	Column II
A. Copper and aluminium	1. Electrodes
B. Tester	2. Good conductor
C. Carbon tod	3. Detect the current
D. Lemon juice	4. Added to water to increase the conductivity

Codes

	A	B	C	D
(a)	2	3	1	4
(b)	1	2	3	4
(c)	4	3	2	1
(d)	2	1	3	4

38. Match the Column I with Column II and choose the correct answer from the codes given below.

	Column I		Column II
A.	Chromium	1.	Food cans
B.	Gold plating	2.	Prevents rusting
C.	Tin	3.	Artificial jewellery
D.	Electroplating	4.	Scratch proof

Codes

	A	B	C	D		A	B	C	D
(a)	2	3	4	1	(b)	4	2	1	3
(c)	4	2	3	1	(d)	4	3	1	2

39. Which of the following statements is/are correct?

I. Electrolyte is more conducting than metal.
II. Ions move slow than electrons.
III. Rain water is a conductor of electricity.
IV. If a little salt is dissolved to the distilled water, it becomes good conductor of electricity.

Codes

(a) I and II (b) III and IV
(c) I, II and III (d) II, III and IV

40. Match the Column I with Column II and choose the correct answer from the codes given below.

	Column I		Column II
A.	Movement of charge through a body	1.	Voltmeter
B.	Electrode connected to negative	2.	Electrolysis
C.	Used in purification of metal	3.	Cathode
D.	Apparatus for electrolysis	4.	Electric Current

Codes

	A	B	C	D		A	B	C	D
(a)	1	2	3	4	(b)	4	3	2	1
(c)	4	3	1	2	(d)	1	4	3	2

Chapter 12

Some Natural Phenomenon

1 Mark Questions

1. A trident shaped device on top of tall buildings which provide a low resistance path to the ground and protect buildings from effect of lightning, is called

(a) lightning inductor
(b) lightning conductor
(c) lightning generator
(d) electroscope

2. A thunderstorm is a type of storm characterised by the presence of lightning and thunder. During thunderstorm

(a) negative charges accumulate near lower edges of cloud
(b) negative charges accumulate near upper edges of cloud
(c) negative charges do not accumulate in the cloud
(d) Both (a) and (b) are true

3. Two charged objects are brought close to each other. Choose the most appropriate statement from the following options.

(a) They may attract
(b) They may repel
(c) They may attract or repel depending on the type of charges they carry
(d) There will be no effect

4. Lightning usually occurs within a cloud in the sky and is called sheet lightning. Storm clouds carry electric charges.

Which type of charges are stored in clouds?

(a) Positive
(b) Negative
(c) Neutral
(d) Both (a) and (b)

5. Aman's mother told him not to carry an umbrella during a thunderstorm. Why did she say so?

(a) The umbrella will not withstand the storm
(b) The metal tip of umbrella can attract lightning
(c) The umbrella may break
(d) A raincoat is better than an umbrella

6. Pankhul was driving his car when he got caught in a thunderstorm. What do you suggest that he should do to protect himself?

(a) Get out of the car and take cover under an open shaded area
(b) Run to the nearest tree
(c) Stand near an electric pole
(d) Remain in car

7. Which gas is produced in air during lightning?
   (a) Carbon dioxide (b) Hydrogen
   (c) Ozone (d) Oxygen

8. When, we remove polyester or woolen cloth in dark, we can see spark and hear a cracking sound. These are due to
   (a) static electricity
   (b) current electricity
   (c) reflection of light
   (d) refraction of light

9. During a thunderstorm, an observer can see lightning before hearing its thunder. Why does he see lightning before he hear thunder?
   (a) Sound travels slower than light
   (b) Sound needs a medium to travel through
   (c) Sound cannot reflect off surfaces as easily as light
   (d) Sound is not processed by the brain as fast as light

10. Raman said to his son that it is safer to use mobile phones and cordless phones during a thunderstorm. Why did he say so?
   (a) Because, they are not connected to wires which can be affected by lightning
   (b) Because, we can contact people when we are afraid
   (c) As, they are our connect to the outside world
   (d) None of the above

11. Select the correct statement.
   (a) The process of electric discharge between clouds and the earth or between different clouds causes lightning.
   (b) Lightning conductor can protect buildings from the effect of thunder.
   (c) One end of the lightning rod is kept out in the air and the other is kept open on the ground.
   (d) Electrical lights must be put off during a thunderstorm.

12. The instrument that is used to detect an earthquake is
   (a) anemometer
   (b) electroscope
   (c) barometer
   (d) seismograph

13. Tsunami is also a destructive natural phenomenon which can cause a huge loss of life and property (houses and other buildings, etc.). Which of the following is not likely to cause tsunami?
   (a) A major nuclear explosion under sea
   (b) Earthquake
   (c) Volcanic eruption
   (d) Lightning

14. The structure of Earth consists of three main layers: core, mantle and crust.
   The Earth's plate responsible for causing Earthquake is
   (a) crust (b) mantle
   (c) inner core (d) outer core

15. Consider the list of terms given below.
   I. Seismic zone
   II. Fault zone
   III. Mantle
   IV. Inner core

   The boundaries of the Earth's plate are known as
   (a) I and II
   (b) I and III
   (c) III and IV
   (d) II, III and IV

16. Consider the list of terms given below.

I. Tsunami
II. Landslide
III. Floods
IV. Lightning

Earthquake can cause

(a) I, II and III (b) II and IV
(c) II, III and IV (d) III and IV

17. Which of the following statement(s) is/are correct?

I. The outermost layer of Earth is in one piece.
II. Each fragment of the Earth is called a tectonic plate.
III. Tectonic plates are always at rest.
IV. The boundaries of the plates are the zones where Earthquake occurs.

Codes

(a) I and II (b) II and IV
(c) I and III (d) Only IV

18. Consider the different words given as below.

I. Seismograph
II. Fault lines
III. Electrograph
IV. Richter scale

Pick the odd one out from the above.

(a) I and III (b) Only II
(c) Only III (d) I and IV

2 Marks Questions

19. **Assertion** (A) Tsunamis are a huge catastrophic disaster which can be caused by an Earthquake on the sea floor.

Reason (R) An Earthquake is caused by the movement of tectonic plates.

(a) Both A and R are true and R is the correct explantion of A.
(b) Both A and R are true, but R is not the correct explanation of A.
(c) A is true, but R is false.
(d) A is false, but R is true.

20. State [T] for True and [F] for False.

I. Richter scale is a device which tests whether an object is carrying charge or not.
II. A lightning conductor protects building from the effect of lightning by the process of discharging.
III. A lightning rod must be taller than the structure it is meant for.
IV. In an electrical storm, the upper portion of the cloud is negative and the lower portion is positive.

Codes

	I	II	III	IV		I	II	III	IV
(a)	F	F	T	T	(b)	F	F	T	F
(c)	T	F	F	T	(d)	T	T	F	T

21. State [T] for True and [F] for False.

I. Tides in the ocean cause tsunami.
II. Tsunami is the huge waves created during Earthquake.
III. Earthquakes can be predicted in advance.
IV. The plates of the outermost layer of the earth are always in continuous motion.

Codes

	I	II	III	IV		I	II	III	IV
(a)	T	F	T	F	(b)	F	T	F	T
(c)	T	T	F	F	(d)	F	F	T	T

22. Which of these things would you do if you live in the Earthquake prone area?

I. You would keep an emergency kit always ready.

II. You would have an open book shelves and open cupboards.

III. You would fix the cupboards to the walls.

IV. You would not keep breakable items on the upper shelves.

Codes

(a) Only III is correct
(b) Both I and III are correct
(c) I, III and IV are correct
(d) All of the above

23. Earthquakes at two places *A* and *B* were measured by a seismograph which recorded the magnitude as 2 and 4. He magnitude of tremors and the destructive energy at *A* and *B* can be compared as

(a) tremors at *B* are two times those at place *A*
(b) tremors at *B* are four times those at place *A*
(c) tremors at *B* are 100 times those at place *A*
(d) tremors at *B* are 1000 times those at place *A*

Chapter 13

Light

1 Mark Questions

1. Which of these depict diffused reflection?

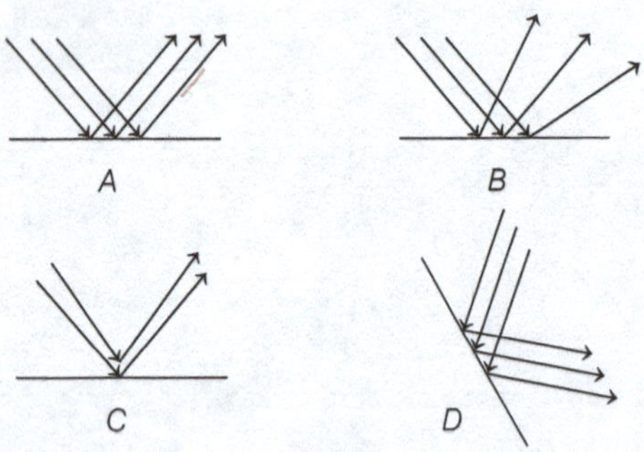

(a) Both *A* and *B* (b) *A*, *B* and *C*
(c) Only *D* (d) Only *B*

2. Which statement is not true in context with the figure given below?

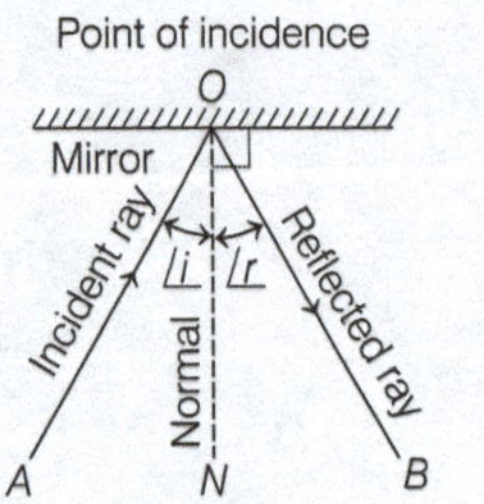

(a) $\angle AON = \angle BON$
(d) *AO* is the incident ray
(c) *O* is the only point from where the light ray can be reflected
(d) If *BO* is the incident ray, then *OA* will be the reflected ray

3. Which of these are characteristics of diffused reflection?

I. Reflected rays go in one direction.
II. Reflected rays are not parallel to each other.
III. It is caused by irregularities of the reflecting surface.

Codes

(a) I and II
(b) II and III
(c) Only I
(d) Only II

4. The figure shows a ray of light reflected at a plane mirror. Which pair of the angles of incidence and angles of reflection is correct?

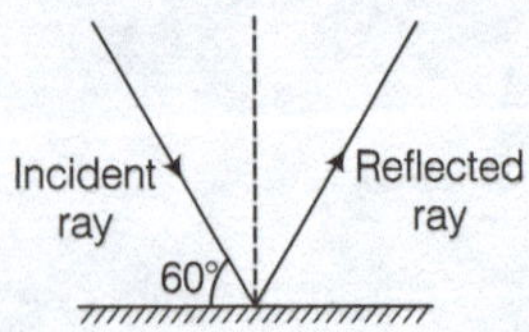

	Angle of incidence	Angle of reflection
(a)	30°	30°
(b)	30°	60°
(c)	60°	30°
(d)	60°	45°

5. A doll is placed between two parallel plane mirrors separated by 60 cm. How many images of the doll will be formed?

(a) 60 (b) 90 (c) 120 (d) Infinite

6. If the angle between incident ray and surface is 40° as shown in figure. What will be the angle of reflection?

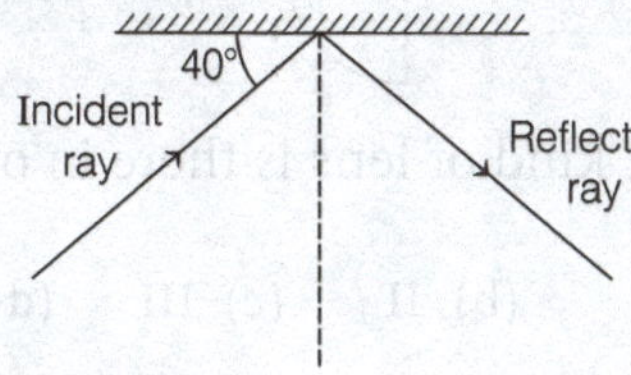

(a) 30° (b) 40°
(c) 50° (d) 60°

7. Light is falling on surfaces S_1, S_2, S_3 as shown in figures

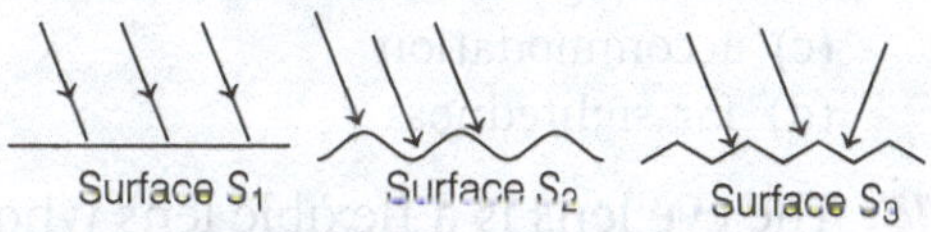

Surfaces on which the angle of incidence is equal to the angle of reflection is/are?

(a) Only S_1
(b) Both S_1 and S_2
(c) Both S_2 and S_3
(d) All the three surfaces

8. The image in a plane mirror is

I. upright.
II. real.
III. the same sized as the object.
IV. as far behind the mirror as the object is in front of it.

Codes

(a) Only I (b) I, II and III
(c) I, III and IV (d) All of these

9. An optician holds a test card 50 cm behind a patient. The patient, then looks in the plane mirror which is 100 cm away. How far away from the patients eye is the image of test card?

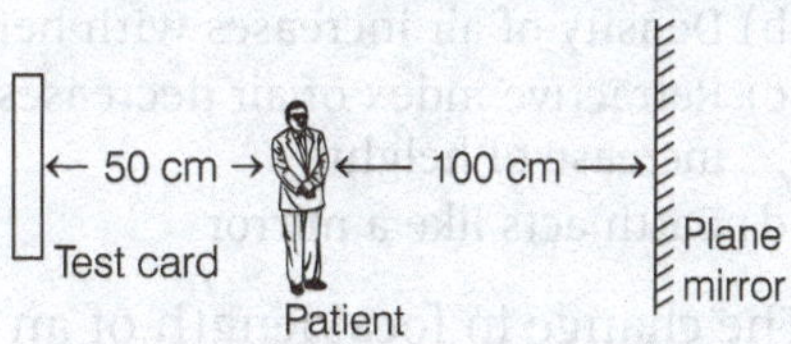

(a) 100 cm (b) 150 cm
(c) 200 cm (d) 250 cm

10. A man looked into a plane mirror and saw the clock as shown. The time on the clock was

(a) 8 : 50 (b) 9 : 10
(c) 3 : 10 (d) 3 : 50

11. Which optical phenomenon is depicted in the figure below?

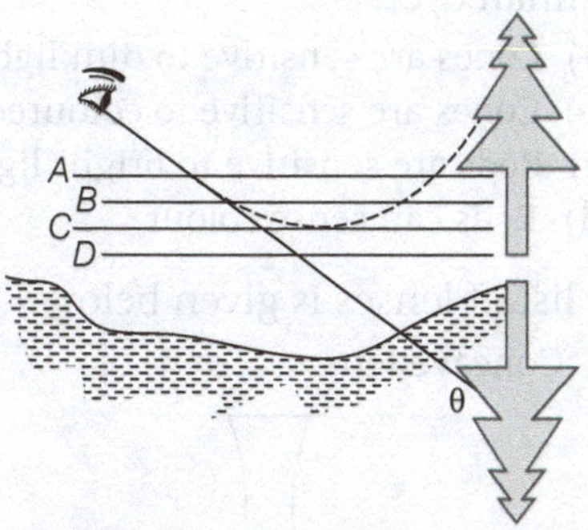

(a) Reflection of light
(b) Dispersion of light
(c) Scattering of light
(d) Refraction of light

12. With reference to the figure shown in above question, what is the cause of this optical illusion?
(a) Density of air decreases with increase of height
(b) Density of air increases with height
(c) Refractive index of air decreases with increase of height
(d) Earth acts like a mirror

13. The change in focal length of an eye lens to focus the image of objects at varying distances is done by the action of
(a) pupil (b) iris
(c) retina (d) ciliary muscles

14. When we enter into a dark room, we cannot see properly for some time. This is because
(a) pupil does not close
(b) pupil does not open
(c) adjustment of size of pupil takes some time
(d) None of the above

15. Which of the following statements is correct regarding rods and cones in human eye?
(a) Cones are sensitive to dim light
(b) Cones are sensitive to coloured light
(c) Rods are sensitive to bright light
(d) Rods can sense colour

16. A list of lenses is given below.
I. Concave lens

II. Convex lens

III. Plano–concave lens

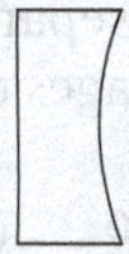

IV. Plano–convex lens

What kind of lens is there in our eyes?
(a) I (b) II (c) III (d) IV

17. The human eye can focus objects at different distances by adjusting the focal length of the eye lens. This is due to
(a) presbyopia
(b) near-sightedness
(c) accommodation
(d) far-sightedness

18. The eye lens is a flexible lens whose thickness and focal length can be changed by the action of ciliary muscles. The focal length of the eye lens increases when eye muscles
(a) are relaxed and lens becomes thicker
(b) contract and lens becomes thicker
(c) are relaxed and lens becomes thinner
(d) contract and lens becomes thinner

19. Which of the following statement(s) about human eye is/are correct?
I. The iris is the outer coat of the eye.
II. It is behind the pupil.
III. Iris controls the adjustment of size of pupil.
IV. Iris is the coloured part of the eye.

Codes
(a) I and II (b) Only II
(c) II and III (d) III and IV

20. State [T] for True and [F] for False.

I. Rods sense colour.
II. Cones are sensitive to bright light.
III. Rods are sensitive to dim light.
IV. Cones function in dim light.

Codes

	I	II	III	IV		I	II	III	IV
(a)	T	T	T	F	(b)	F	F	T	T
(c)	T	F	F	T	(d)	F	T	T	F

21. Which of the following statements is/are correct?

Statement I It is difficult to thread a needle with one eye closed in comparison with keeping both eyes open.

Statement II A human eye cannot see an object clearly for an object placed at a distance smaller than a certain minimum distance.

(a) Only I (b) Only II
(c) Both I and II (d) None of these

22. Which of the following statements is/are correct?

Statement I Cinematography is an application of persistence of vision.

Statement II The retina of human eye has an ability to retain the image of an object for one-sixteenth of a second even after the removal of the object.

(a) Only statement I is correct.
(b) Only statement II is correct.
(c) Both statements are correct.
(d) Both statements are incorrect.

2 Marks Questions

23. A list of objects is given below.

(i) Sun (ii) Moon (iii) Earth (iv) Stars (v) Glowing tubelight (vi) Table (vii) Fire

Category I Luminous objects
Category II Non-luminous objects

What is the correct division of the given list of objects according to the two categories given?

(a) I : (i), (ii), (iii), (iv)
II : (v), (vi), (vii)
(b) I : (i), (iv), (v), (vii)
II : (ii), (iii), (vi)
(c) I : (i), (ii), (iv)
II : (iii), (v), (vi), (vii)
(d) I : (i), (iv), (vii)
II : (ii), (iii), (v), (vi)

24. Match the Column I with Column II.

Column I	Column II
A. Point of incidence	1. Ray of light which is incident on the surface of mirror.
B. Reflected ray	2. Perpendicular drawn at the point of incidence.
C. Incident ray	3. Ray of light which bounces off the mirror.
D. Normal at the point of incidence	4. Point where the incident ray strikes the surface of the mirror.

Codes

	A	B	C	D		A	B	C	D
(a)	4	3	1	2	(b)	1	3	2	4
(c)	3	4	1	2	(d)	4	1	2	3

25. State [T] for True and [F] for False.

I. Dispersion of light causes rainbow.

II. Diffused reflection of light occurs due to failure of the laws of reflection.

III. Image formed by a plane mirror is always laterally inverted.

Codes

	I	II	III		I	II	III
(a)	T	T	T	(b)	T	F	T
(c)	F	T	T	(d)	T	F	F

26. Match the Column I with Column II.

Column I	Column II
A. Diffused Reflection	1. Smooth surface
B. Regular reflection	2. Three plane mirror strips inclined at 60° to one another
C. Periscope	3. Irregular surface
D. Kaleidoscope	4. Two plane mirrors arranged parallel to one another

Codes

	A	B	C	D
(a)	1	3	2	4
(b)	1	3	4	2
(c)	3	1	2	4
(d)	3	1	4	2

27. State [T] for True and [F] for False.

I. A person of 1m long in front of a plane mirror seems to be 1 m from the image.

II. If you touch your left ear with right hand in front of a plane mirror, it will be seen in the mirror that your right ear is touched with left hand.

III. Splitting of white light into its constituent colours is known as diffraction.

IV. According to the laws of reflection, $\angle i$ less than $\angle r$.

Codes

	I	II	III	IV		I	II	III	IV
(a)	T	F	T	F	(b)	T	T	F	F
(c)	T	F	T	T	(d)	T	T	T	F

28. Match the Column I with Column II.

Column I	Column II
A. Cataract	1. Junction of optic nerve and retina
B. Cornea	2. Cloudy eye lens
C. Blind spot	3. 1/16th of a second
D. Persistence of vision	4. Front part of eye

Codes

	A	B	C	D		A	B	C	D
(a)	4	1	3	2	(b)	4	2	1	3
(c)	2	4	1	3	(d)	2	4	3	1

29. State [T] for True and [F] for False.

I. The most comfortable distance of clear reading with normal vision is approximately 25 cm.

II. The size of the pupil becomes small when you see in dim light.

III. Night birds have more cones than rods in their eyes.

IV. The image is formed at retina of an eye.

V. Cinematography works on the principle of reflection of light.

Codes

	I	II	III	IV	V
(a)	T	F	F	T	F
(b)	T	F	T	F	T
(c)	F	F	T	T	F
(d)	F	T	F	F	F

PRACTICE SET 01

1 Mark Questions

1. Which of the following factors affect the natural habitat of endemic species?

I. Destruction of their habitat.
II. Increasing human population.
III. Introduction of new species.
IV. Introduction of same species.

(a) I and II
(b) II and III
(c) I, II and III
(d) I, II, III and IV

2. Match the Column I with Column II.

	Column I (Position of object)		Column I (Position of image
A.	Between focus and centre of curvature.	1.	At infinity
B.	Between pole and focus	2.	At centre of curvature
C.	At focus	3.	Behind the mirror
D.	At centre of curvature	4.	Beyond C

Codes

	A	B	C	D
(a)	4	3	1	2
(b)	3	4	2	1
(c)	4	1	3	2
(d)	3	4	1	2

3. The given below diagram shows a rubber tyre.

There are deep treads on the tyre because they

(a) increase the slipping distance of the car
(b) reduce the amount of material used
(c) enable the tyre to move smoothly
(d) increase friction

4. The following diagram shows an oil well with natural gas, oil and water.

Oil and gas form the upper layer. This is because

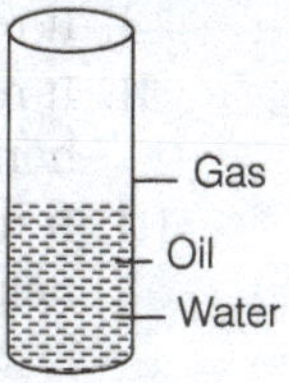

Oil well

(a) these are heavier than water
(b) these are lighter than water
(c) these get stick to each other
(d) these mix with water

5. The force of friction between two bodies is

(a) parallel to the contact surfaces
(b) perpendicular to the contact surfaces
(c) inclined at 30° to the contact surfaces
(d) inclined at 60° to the contact surfaces

6. **Statement I** Pressure is defined as the force acting per unit length of the surface.

Statement II Force acting perpendicular to the surface is called thrust.

(a) Statement I is correct.
(b) Statement II is correct.
(c) Statements I and II are correct.
(d) Both the statements are incorrect.

7. Which of the following is the best thing to do during heavy lightning?
(a) Lying on the ground in an open place
(b) Going into the nearest water body
(c) Staying indoors away from metallic doors or windows
(d) Standing under a tall tree

8. Look at the figure and their functions given below.

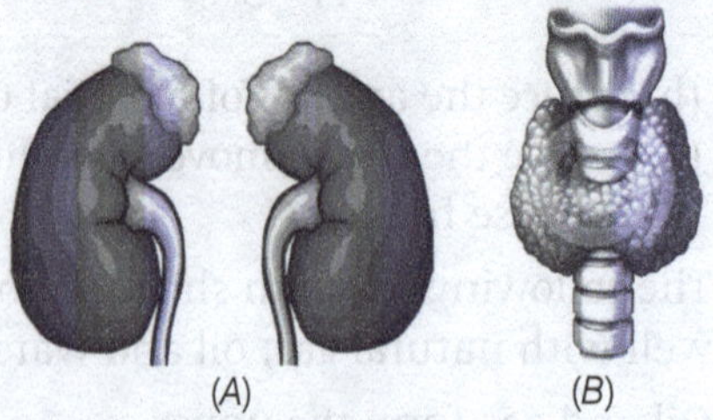

I. It releases the growth hormones
II. It releases T_3 and T_4 (thyroxin) hormone.
III. It releases adrenalin hormones which helps in increase the body's energy level.

Codes
(a) *A* – Adrenal glands – I, *B* – Thyroid gland – II
(b) *A* – Adrenal glands – III, *B* – Thyroid gland – II
(c) *A* – Thyroid gland – II, *B* – Adrenal gland – III
(d) *A* – Thyroid gland – II, *B* – Pituitary gland – I

9. Match the following columns.

	Column I		Column II
A.	Point of incidence	1.	Ray of light which is incident on the surface of mirror
B.	Reflected ray	2.	Perpendicular drawn at the point of incidence
C.	Incident ray	3.	Ray of light which bounces off the mirror
D.	Normal at the point of incidence	4.	Point where the incident ray strikes the surface of the mirror

Codes

	A	B	C	D
(a)	4	3	1	2
(b)	1	3	2	4
(c)	3	4	1	2
(d)	4	1	2	3

10. The frequency of the sound travelling with a velocity of 480 m/sec and a wavelength of 6 m is
(a) 80 Hz (b) 9800 Hz
(c) 2880 Hz (d) 60 Hz

11. A man sharpens his knife as shown in the figure. Which of these properties of friction are in use?

I. Friction helps us to hold objects.
II. Friction acts in the opposite direction of motion.
III. Friction causes the surfaces in contact to wear away.
IV. Friction produces heat energy.

Codes
(a) I and II (b) I, III and IV
(c) III and IV (d) I, II and III

12. Which of the following are negative effects of deforestation on the environment?
I. Destruction of the ozone layer.
II. Erosion of the topsoil.
III. Increase in carbon dioxide level.

Codes
(a) Only I (b) Only II
(c) II and III (d) I, II and III

13. Some students were performing experiment in the laboratory. One step of their experiment involve heating of alcohol. However, their science teacher strictly instructed them not to heat the alcohol directly on the flame.

Why do you think, the teacher gave such an instruction?

I. The temperature of the flame is not high enough to heat the alcohol.
II. Alcohol is highly inflammable substance.
III. The heat of the flame is sufficient to overcome the ignition temperature of alcohol, so it can easily catch fire.

The correct reason(s) is/are

(a) I and II (b) II and III
(c) I and III (d) Only III

14. In human beings, the correct sequence of events of reproduction is

(a) embryo → fertilisation → gamete → gamete formation
(b) Gamete formation → fertilisation → zygote → embryo
(c) fertilisation → gamete formation → embryo → zygote
(d) Gamete formation → fertilisation → embryo → zygote

15. To avoid slipping while walking on ice, we should take smaller steps because

(a) frictional force of ice is large
(b) of larger normal reaction
(c) frictional force of ice is small
(d) of smaller normal reaction

16. If the focal length of a convex lens is 75 cm, what will be the power of the lens.

(a) 1.33 D (b) 1.17 D
(c) 2.0 D (d) 2.5 D.

17. In our human body, 'X' is a gland which is located just below the stomach and secrets a hormone 'Y'. The deficiency of hormone 'Y' in the body causes a disease 'Z' in which blood sugar level of a person gets high.

	X	Y	Z
(a)	Pancrease	Insulin	Diabetes
(b)	Gastric	Estrogen	Thyroid
(c)	Adrenal	Thyroid stimulating Hormone (TSH)	Thyroid
(d)	Pancreas	Insulin	Sugar

18. Some gases are given to you.

Identify the gas(es) which combines with haemoglobin in our blood to form carboxy-haemoglobin and rendering it incapable to combine with oxygen & transport it in our body and cause health issue.

I. Carbon monoxide
II. Carbon dioxide
III. Sulphur dioxide
IV. Nitrogen oxide

Codes

(a) Only I (b) I and II
(c) II and III (d) All of these

19. What benefit does yeast gains from carrying out fermentation?

(a) Carbon dioxide is available for photosynthesis
(b) Energy is available for growth
(c) Ethanol is available for growth
(d) Glucose is available for respiration

20. Radha was cooking the food in the kitchen. She make poori, suddenly cooking oil caught fire. She put water to extinguish the fire but the oil continued to burn with high flames. Explain the reason why?

I. Oil is heavier than water.
II. Water sinks while oil stays on the top and keeps burning.
III. Oil sinks while water stays on the top and hence keeps burning.
IV. Oil is higher than water

Choose the correct option.
(a) Both I and II
(b) Both II and IV
(c) Both I and III
(d) Both II and III

21. Select the correct statement.
(a) The force of friction depends on the area of the surfaces in contact
(b) Rolling friction is less than sliding friction
(c) More the weight, less the frictional force.
(d) Friction produces energy

22. The correct sequence and components of crude oil after fractional distillation of petroleum is

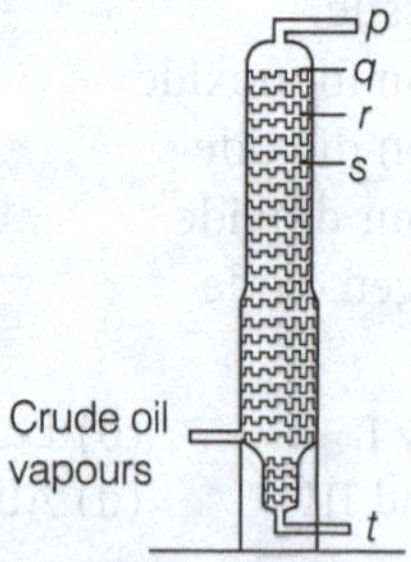

(a) *p*–Residue, *q*–Gasoline, *r*–Petroleum gases, *s*–Kerosene, *t*–Diesel oil
(b) *p*–Petroleum gases, *q*–Gasoline, *r*–Diesel oil, *s*–Kerosene, *t*–Residue
(c) *p*–Petroleum gases, *q*–Gasoline, *r*–Kerosene, *s*–Diesel oil, *t*–Residue
(d) *p*–Petroleum gases, *q*–Kerosene, *r*–Gasoline, *s*–Diesel oil, *t*–Residue

23. Consider the given statements and opt the option that correctly declares them true (T) or false (F).
I. Sodium bicarbonate is an antibiotic.
II. The first antibiotic called penicillin was extracted from fungus.
III. Sodium hydroxide can be used as a food preservative.
IV. Fungus are normally considered as saprophytes.

Codes

	I	II	III	IV
(a)	F	T	F	T
(b)	T	T	F	T
(c)	F	T	T	F
(d)	T	T	T	T

24. The four activities (*A*, *B*, *C* and *D*) below show forces at work.

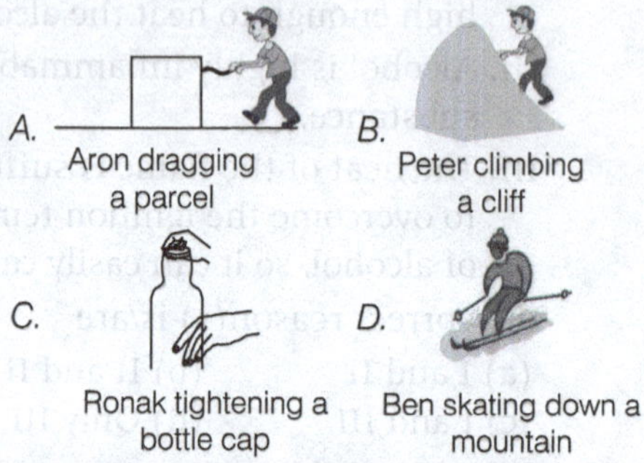

Which of the following activities require the presence of frictional force?
(a) Activities *A* and *B*
(b) Activities *B* and *C*
(c) Activities *A* and *C*
(d) All the activities

25. Fill in the following blanks with the help of codes given below.
The ___(*A*)___ of fossil fuels produces ___(*B*)___. This gas ___(*C*)___ infrared radiation and is also called as __(*D*)__.
What are *A*, *B*, *C* and *D*?

	A	*B*	*C*	*D*
(a)	combustion	CO_2	absorbs	global warming
(b)	increase	carbon dioxide gas	emit	global warming
(c)	ignition	nitrogen	traps	green house gas
(d)	combustion	carbon dioxide gas	traps	green house gas

26. Some Rabi and Kharif crops are given below.
Maize, paddy, cotton, tomato, oats, gram, mustard, wheat, barley.
How many of the following can be considered as Rabi crops?
(a) 6 (b) 5 (c) 3 (d) 4

27. Refer to the given Venn diagram and choose the correct option for X and Y.

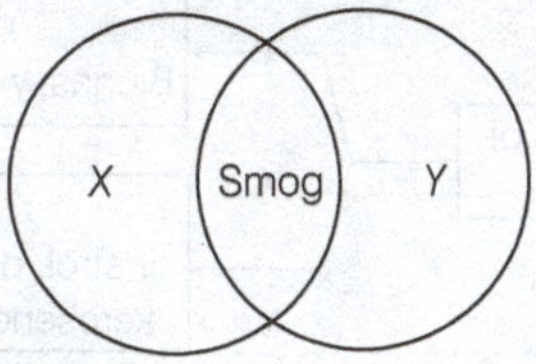

	X	**Y**
(a)	Fire	Water
(b)	Smoke	Fog
(c)	Water	Smoke
(d)	Air	Water

28. Sharad and Sharnav performed experiments taking similar bulbs and cells but two different liquid A and B, respectively, as shown in the given figure. They found that the bulb in the set-up 'A' glows more brightly as compared to set-up B. You would conclude that

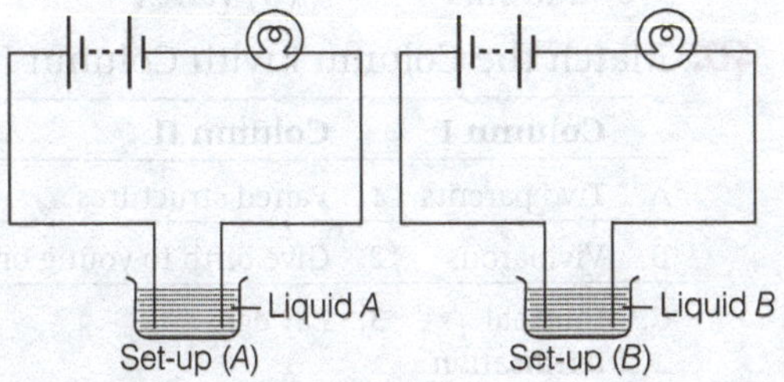

(a) higher current is flowing through the circuit in set-up A
(b) higher current is flowing through the circuit in set-up B
(c) equal current is flowing through both the circuits
(d) the current flowing through the circuits in the two set-ups cannot be compared in this manner

29. Which of the following statements about friction is correct?
(a) Friction can be increased by moisture on the surface
(b) Motion opposes friction
(c) It is not possible to write without friction
(d) Solids and liquids do not allow things to move in or over them

30. Complete the life cycle of a frog using suitable codes given below–

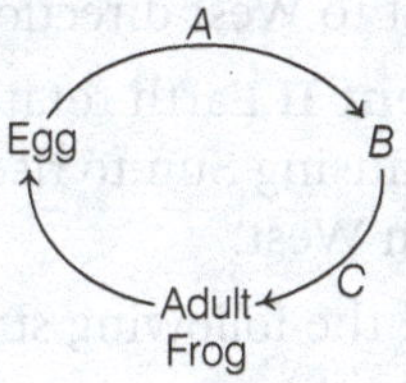

Codes

	A	**B**	**C**
(a)	Metamorphosis	Hatching	Tadpole
(b)	Hatching	Tadpole	Metamorphosis
(c)	Tadpole	Hatching	Metamorphosis
(d)	Metamorphosis	Tadpole	Hatching

31. Which of the following is an example of a single cell that does not function as a full-fledged organism?
A. White Blood Cell (WBC)
B. *Amoeba*
C. WBC and *Amoeba*
D. *Paramecium*
(a) Only B (b) B and D
(c) Only A (d) C and D

32. **Statement I** Fertilisers are used to increase the soil fertility.
Statement II *Rhizobium* is a nitrogen fixation bacteria.
Codes
(a) Only statement I is correct
(b) Only statement II is correct
(c) Both statement I and II are correct
(d) Both statement I and II are incorrect

33. Which of the following statement is incorrect?

(a) Alcohol is produced with the help of yeast

(b) The food material which is preserved by pasteurisation is fruits and vegetables

(c) The bread dough rises because of increased CO_2

(d) The percentage of nitrogen gas in the atmosphere remains constant

34. **Statement I** Stars appear to move from East to West direction.

Statement II Earth rotates from West to East causing Sun to rise from East and set in West.

Which of the following statement(s) is/are correct?

(a) Only I (b) Only II

(c) Both I and II (c) None of these

35. Match the Column I with Column II.

Column I	Column II
A. Coal	1. Bus
B. Water in a dam	2. Thermal power station
C. CNG	3. Hydroelectric power station
D. Wind	4. Cooking
E. LPG	5. Wind mill

Codes

	A	B	C	D	E
(a)	1	2	3	4	5
(b)	2	3	5	4	1
(c)	2	3	1	5	4
(d)	3	1	2	5	4

36. Which of the following algae is used in making glasses and porcelain?

(a) *Chlorella* (b) Diatoms

(c) Green algae (d) *Volvox*

37. Select the incorrect statement.

(a) Angle of incidence is always equal to the angle of reflection

(b) In an image formed by a mirror the left of the object appears on the right and *vice-versa*. This is known as lateral inversion

(c) Reflection from a smooth surface is called diffused reflection

(d) Cone cells sense colours

38. Sources of energy are classified into two categories *X* and *Y* as shown below.

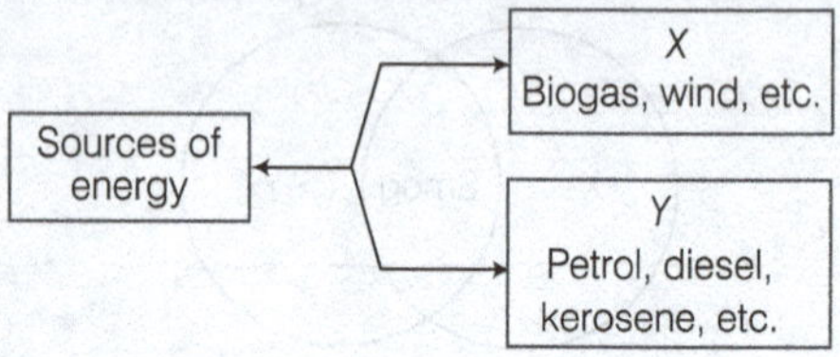

Which of these will go in *Y*?

(a) Liquefied Petroleum Gas

(b) Tides

(c) Coke

(d) All of the above

39. The microorganism in the given figure is

(a) bread mould (b) *penicillin*

(c) diatoms (d) *volvox*

40. Match the Column I with Column II.

Column I	Column II
A. Two parents	1. Paired structures
B. Viviparous	2. Give birth to young ones
C. Internal fertilisation	3. Lay eggs
D. Oviparous	4. Human beings
E. Ovaries	5. Sexual reproduction

Codes

	A	B	C	D	E
(a)	1	5	2	4	3
(b)	5	2	4	3	1
(c)	2	1	3	4	5
(d)	5	4	2	3	1

2 Marks Questions

41. Refer to the given figures showing different microorganisms. Select the correct option regarding the disease caused by these microorganisms.

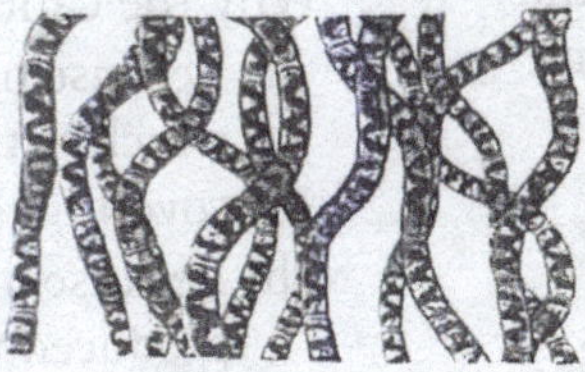

(A)

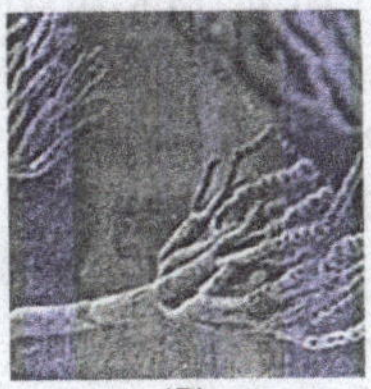

(B)

	A	B
(a) Microorganism Disease -	Bacteria Chicken pox	Protozoa Polio
(b) Microorganism Disease -	Algae Paralytic shellfish poisoning	Fungi Ringworm
(c) Microorganism Disease -	Bacteria Typhoid	Virus Polio
(d) Microorganism Disease -	Fungi Ringworm	Protozoa Polio

42. Fill in the blanks in the table describing some common plant diseases caused by microorganisms.

Plant diseases	Microorganism	Mode of transmission	Figures
(*A*)	Bacteria	(*B*)	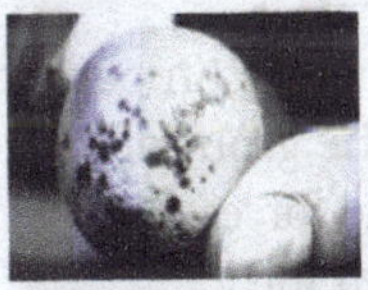
(Rust of wheat)	(*C*)	Air, seeds	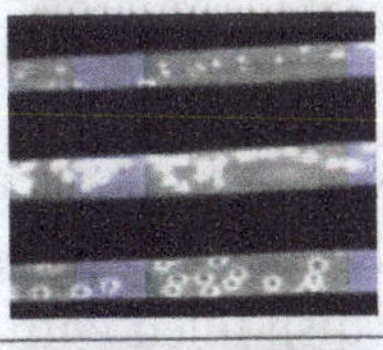
(*D*)	(Virus)	Insect	

Codes

	A	*B*	*C*	*D*
(a)	Scales	Water	Algae	Yellow vein mosaic
(b)	Aster yellows	Air	Algae	Yellow vain mosaic
(c)	Citrus canker	Water	Fungi	Okra
(d)	Citrus canker	Air	Fungi	Okra

43. Parachute works because of air friction. If there was no air friction, then gravity would cause everything to fall at the same rate, so no matter what item you dropped like a feather or a rock it would hit the ground exactly at the same time (assuming you dropped it from the same height). But air friction complicates things.

Air friction comes into action because as things fall, they have to push their way past the atoms and molecules that make up air in order to get their way to proceed.

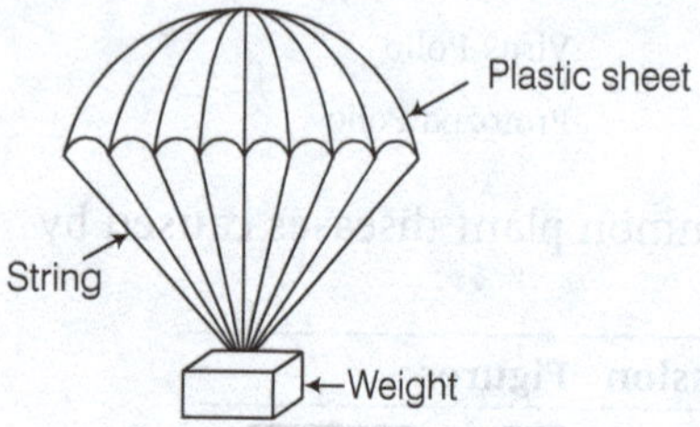

What force acting on parachute caused it to fall to the ground?

(a) Magnetic force
(b) Frictional force
(c) Gravitational force
(d) Both (b) and (c)

44. Ravi took two candles, one smaller and other slightly taller. He placed both the candles in a dish filled with baking soda and the dish is now placed in a large bowl as shown below.

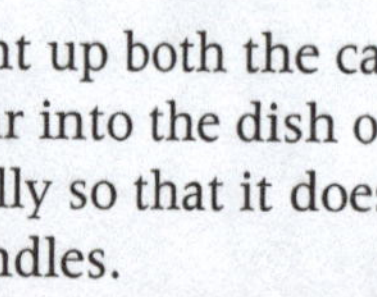

He now light up both the candles and pour vinegar into the dish of baking soda carefully so that it does not fall over the candles.

After some time, he observed that both the candles get extinguished. First smaller candle extinguish and later the larger one.

Why the candles get extinguished?

(a) Because of the production of water which cuts the supply of air by covering the fire
(b) Because of carbon dioxide gas produced which cuts the supply of air (oxygen) by covering the fire
(c) Because of nitrogen gas produced, which cuts the supply of air by covering the fire
(d) Both (a) and (b)

45. Mohan, a poor farmer has only one crop field and weeds are growing in his field. He is worrying about that the weedicides continuously damages the crop. So, in order to stop the damage he wants to spray the field.

Given below, the time period are shown–

Choose the correct time where the weedicide spray is most effective.

(a) Mohan should spray his field at the time of full growth of weeds
(b) Spray before flowering and seed forming
(c) He should spray after flowering
(d) None of above is effective

46. Under normal working conditions, radio loudspeakers, industrial machinery and children in a playground, all produce sound waves. Under the same air conditions, all these sound waves

(a) have the same amplitude
(b) have the same frequency
(c) have the same wavelength
(d) travel with same speed

47. In order to show the classification of fossil fuels, Mr. Verma, the science teacher draw the following flowchart.

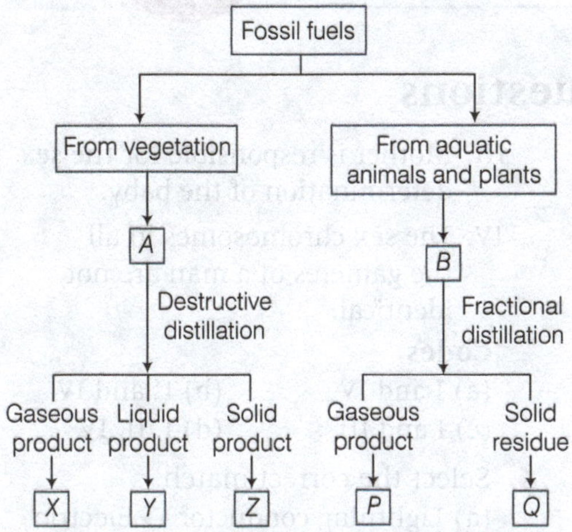

The set showing correct match for the vacant spaces (A, B, X, Y, Z, P and Q) is
(a) A = Petroleum, Y = Coal tar, Q = Coke
(b) X = Coal gas, Z = Coke, Q = Bitumen
(c) B = Petroleum, Z = Coke, P = Gasoline
(d) A = Coal, X = Coal tar, Q = Gasoline

48. Match the column I with column II.

	Column I		Column II
A.	AIDS	1.	Fungus
B.	Ringworm	2.	Protozoa
C.	Malaria	3.	Virus
D.	Whooping cough	4.	Bacteria

Codes

	A	B	C	D		A	B	C	D
(a)	1	3	4	2	(b)	2	4	3	1
(c)	3	1	2	4	(d)	3	2	4	1

49. The species A and B of wild animals are found only in a particular are. The species C of wild animals is no longer exist. While the species D is mentioned in Red data book of India.

Identify A, B, C and D from the codes–

	A	*B*	*C*	*D*
(a)	Endemic	Endemic	Extinct	Endangered
(b)	Extinct	Endangered	Endemic	Endangered
(c)	Endemic	Endemic	Extinct	Extinct
(d)	Endangered	Endangered	Extinct	Endemic

50. When a motor with iron wheel is pushed to roll on iron rails, it travels more distance than when a similar motor with rubber tyres pushed with same force. The reason is the rolling friction in the iron is lesser than the rubber. Why?

Choose the correct answer.
(a) Because of fluid friction due to air pressure of rubber tyres
(b) Rubber tyre increase the resistive force
(c) The less friction between iron wheel and iron rails
(d) None of the above

PRACTICE SET 02

1 Mark Questions

1. Match the Column I with Column II.

Column I		Column II	
A.	Frictional force	1.	Comb with dry hair
B.	Electrostatic force	2.	Bullock pulling cart
C.	Muscular force	3.	Rolling ball
D.	Gravitational force	4.	Apple falling from tree

Codes

	A	B	C	D		A	B	C	D
(a)	1	4	3	2	(b)	2	3	1	4
(c)	3	1	2	4	(d)	3	2	1	4

2. Rahul pushes a wall for a very long time and gets tired. His muscles started aching but he still couldn't move the wall.

Which among the following statement is correct?

I. No work is done by Rahul.
II. Rahul spends a lot of his energy.
III. Wall is stationary and cannot be moved.
IV. Wall has a very ligh static friction.

Codes

(a) Only I
(b) Only II
(c) I, II and IV
(d) I, II, III and IV

3. Which of the following is/are correct?

I. Testes are responsible for production of sperms.
II. Stoppage of menstruation is called adolescence.
III. Mother is responsible for the sex determination of the baby.
IV. The sex chromosomes in all the gametes of a man are not identical.

Codes

(a) I and IV (b) II and IV
(c) I and III (d) I, II, IV

4. Select the correct match.

(a) Lightning conductor → Electric current
(b) Seismic zones → Weak
(c) Moving charges → Earthquake
(d) Earth's plate → Protection

5. Match the items given in Column I with their most suitable match given in Column II and choose the correct answer using the codes given below.

Column I	Column II
A. LPG	1. Plastic
B. CNG	2. Petroleum gas in liquid form
C. Conversion of coal into coke	3. Natural gas
D. Petroleum	4. Coal gas
	5. Produces gas

Codes

	A	B	C	D
(a)	4	3	5	1
(b)	2	3	5	1
(c)	2	4	5	1
(d)	2	3	4	1

6. Match the items given in Column I with those in Column II suitably.

Column I	Column II
A. Satpura	1. Protect animals
B. Deforestation	2. Killing of animals
C. Global warming	3. Cutting of trees
D. Poaching	4. National park
E. Zoo	5. Increasing carbon dioxide

Codes

	A	B	C	D	E
(a)	4	3	5	2	1
(b)	1	2	3	4	5
(c)	5	4	3	2	1
(d)	1	2	4	3	5

7. Which of the following cannot be charged easily by friction?
(a) A plastic scale
(b) A copper rod
(c) An inflated balloon
(d) A woollen cloth

8. When hot air is passed through the coke, the following reaction takes place.

$$\text{Coke} \xrightarrow{\text{Hot air}} \underset{\text{Non-poisonous}}{A} + \underset{\text{Poisonous}}{B}$$

Increased concentration of A is a cause of
I. acid rain
II. global warming
III. greenhouse effect

The correct answer(s) is/are
(a) I and II (b) II and III
(c) Only II (d) I, II and III

9. State [T] for True and [F] for False.
I. External fertilisation can occur both in water and on land.
II. The eggs of fish are covered by hard shells for protection.
III. Human egg has a head, middle piece and tail.
IV. In adult human females, a single mature egg is released into an oviduct every month.

Codes

	I	II	III	IV		I	II	III	IV
(a)	F	F	F	T	(b)	F	F	T	F
(c)	T	F	F	T	(d)	F	T	F	T

10. Which of the following statements is/are correct?
I. The same kind of plants grown and cultivated on a large scale at a place is called crop.
II. The first step before growing crops is preparation of the soil.
III. Damaged seeds would float on top of water.
IV. For growing a crop, sufficient sunlight, water and nutrients from the soil are essential.

Codes
(a) II and III (b) I and IV
(c) Only III (d) All of these

11. Match the terms in Column I with those of Column II.

Column I	Column II
A. Friction	1. Measuring force
B. Spring balance	2. Reduce friction
C. Shape of aeroplane	3. Nature of surface
D. Lubricants	4. Drag
E. Fluid friction	5. Bird

Codes

	A	B	C	D	E
(a)	5	4	3	2	1
(b)	3	1	5	2	4
(c)	1	2	3	4	5
(d)	4	3	5	1	2

12. The focus is also called the hypocentre of an earthquake. The vibrating waves travel away from the focus of the earthquake in all directions. Directly above the focus on the Earth's surface is the earthquake's epicentre. Earthquake waves do not originate at epicentre.

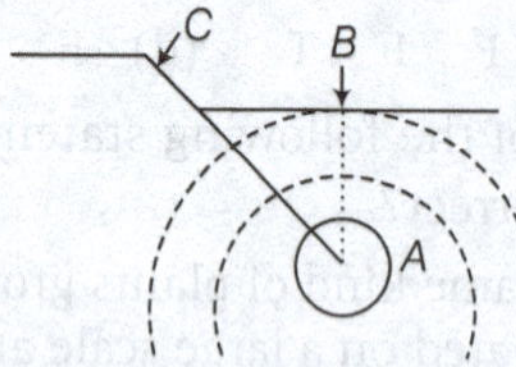

Point *A* where slip initiated during the earthquake is called the ....

(a) dip (b) epicentre

(c) focus (d) scarp

13. What force acting on parachute keeps it afloat for a few seconds before falling to the ground?

(a) Magnetic force

(b) Frictional force

(c) Gravitational force

(d) Both (b) and (c)

14. When several molecules of *X* are combined with several molecules of *Y*, a product is obtained, structure of which is given below.

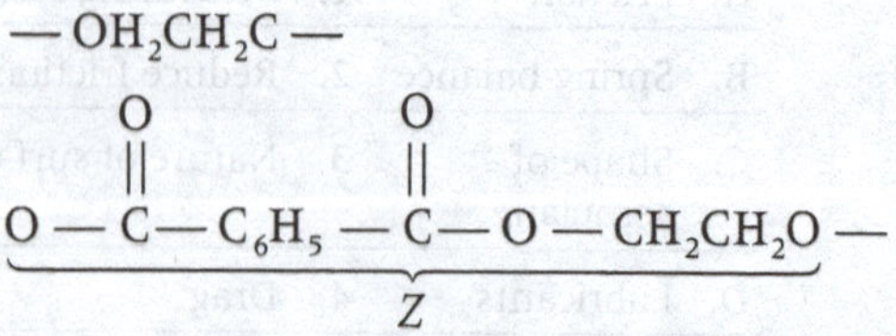

The unit *Z* here represents a

(a) polymer (b) monomer

(c) repeating unit (d) None of these

15. What may result when the environment becomes unfavourable to the organisms?

I. The organisms may die.

II. The organisms may adapt.

III. The organisms may move to another place.

(a) I and II (b) II and III

(c) I and III (d) I, II and III

16. Three glass jars *P*, *Q* and *R* filled with carbon dioxide, sulphur dioxide and oxygen gases respectively. In each jar, a lighted candle is placed simultaneously. In which jar, will the candle remain lighted for a longer time.

(a) In jar *P* (b) In jar *Q*

(c) In jar *R* (d) None of these

17. Metamorphosis is a reproduction process that involves transformation, opt the option that correctly defines the metamorphosis in butterfly.

(a) Pupa → Adult

(b) Larva → Adult

(c) Egg → Adult

(d) Adult butterfly emerging from pupa and egg

18. Match the Column I with Column II.

	Column I		Column II
A.	Friction produces	1.	Ceiling fan
B.	Wheels	2.	More friction
C.	Ball bearing	3.	Heat
D.	Rough surface	4.	Rolling friction

Codes

	A	B	C	D
(a)	4	3	1	2
(b)	3	4	2	1
(c)	3	4	1	2
(d)	4	1	2	3

19. Forces are invisible but they can be ....

A. felt B. heard

C. seen in action D. measured

(a) A and B (b) A and C

(c) A, C and D (d) A, B, C and D

20. Which of the following organisms are protected in Rann of Kutch Wildlife Sanctuary?

A. Wild ass B. Flamingo
C. Desert fox D. Asiatic lion

(a) B and C (b) A and D
(c) A, B and C (d) A, B, C and D

21. Sparks can be seen on the electric poles, due to which wire becomes.

(a) loose (b) tight
(c) wrinkle (d) None of these

22. Which one of the following human activities has a negative impact on the environment?

(a) Recycling
(b) Reforestation
(c) Usage of chlorofluorocarbon (CFC) products
(d) Developing energy efficient technology

23. Some of the friendly and harmful microorganisms are given in box.

Yeast, Malarial Parasite, *Lactobacillus*, Bread Mould, *Rhizobium*, *Bacillius anthracis*

How many of them are harmful microorganisms?

(a) 4 (b) 3
(c) 5 (d) 2

24. Lightning may appears in ……… cycle.

(a) nitrogen (b) water
(c) carbon (d) electrical

25. Since, ancient time, *X* has been used for the large scale production of alcoholic drinks such as wine. The conversion of sugar to alcohol is known as *Y*.

Identify the process *Y*.

(a) Decantation (b) Fermentation
(c) Decomposition (d) Distillation

26. **Statement I** Formation of coal, petroleum and natural gas required a very high temperature and pressure.

Statement II Coal, petroleum and natural gas can be prepared in the laboratory.

Which of the following statement(s) is/are correct?

(a) Only 1 (b) Only II
(c) Both I and II (d) None of these

27. A spring balance was used to measure the force needed to pull a wooden block across different surfaces. The table shows the results. The force is expressed in Newton. In which of the following is the friction greatest?

Floor surface	Force needed to just start moving
Carpet	10 N
Polished tiles	2 N
Polished wood	5 N
Thick rug	12 N

(a) Carpet
(b) Polished tiles
(c) Polished wood
(d) Thick rug

28. Air is a mixture of various gases. One of the gases is 21% part of the air and is essential for the survival of human beings. This gas is……… .

(a) nitrogen (b) oxygen
(c) ozone (d) argon

29. Lightning can be seen at the moment when it occurs. Seema observes lightning in her area. She is at 1980 m distance where the lightning occurs. How long after lightning will Seema hear the sound?

(a) 5s (b) 6s
(c) 7s (d) 4s

30. Which of the following are the fractions of petroleum.

I. Petrol II. Lubricating oil
III. Kerosene IV. Paraffin wax

Codes

(a) I and III (b) I, II and III
(c) II and IV (d) All of these

31. State [T] for True and [F] for False.

I. An electric current can produce chemical, heating and magnetic effects.
II. Plastic wire is an insulator.
III. The water and acid solution can not conduct electricity.
IV. The presence of a small amount of impurities makes water a good conductor of electricity.

Codes

	I	II	III	IV
(a)	T	T	F	T
(b)	T	T	F	F
(c)	F	T	F	T
(d)	F	T	F	T

32. A pendulum oscillates 50 times in 5s. Find its time period.

(a) 10 s (b) $\frac{1}{10}$ s
(c) 20 s (d) $\frac{1}{20}$ s

33. Which of the following is/are correct?

I. Angle of incident is greater than the angle of reflection.
II. The image formed by a plane mirror is real.
III. Cones and rods are the light sensitive cells.
IV. Two mirrors inclined to each other give multiple images.

Codes

(a) I and IV (b) II, III and IV
(c) III and IV (d) Only II

34. Rahul was observing colour of flames produced by different sources.

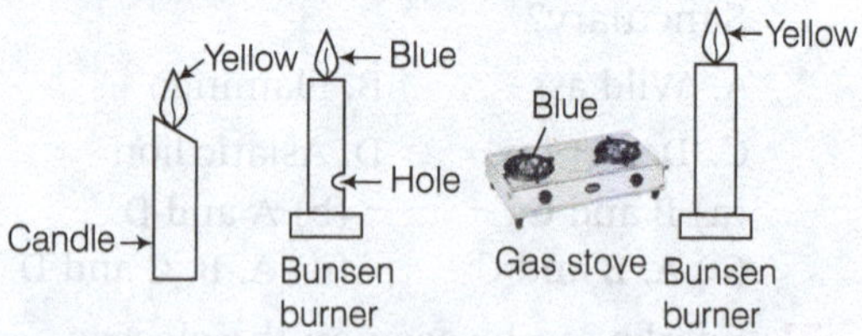

On the basis of his observations, he concluded that the colour of the flame depends upon

I. the substance burning in the flame.
II. the amount of oxygen available for combustion.
III. quantity of source used.
IV. temperature of the flame.

The correct observations are

(a) I, II and III (b) I and II
(c) II and III (d) I, II and IV

35. The teacher asked the children to make a statement about friction. Which of the student spoke correctly?

Alan Friction holds a nail in a wall.
Ayush Ball bearing help to increase friction.
Kavita We can reduce friction.
Anjana Life would be easy without friction.

(a) Alan and Ayush
(b) Alan and Kavita
(c) Ayush and Kavita
(d) Anjana and Ayush

36. An archer stretches his bow while taking aim at the target he then releases the arrow, which begins to move towards the target. Based on this information which of the following statements are correct?

I. To stretch the bow, the archer applies a force that causes a change in its shape.

II. The force applied by the archer to stretch the bow is an example of friction force.

III. The type of force responsible for a change in the state of motion of the arrow is an example of a contact force.

IV. While the arrow moves towards its target, the forces acting on it are due to gravity and that due to friction of air.

Codes

(a) I, II, III (b) III and IV

(c) I, III and IV (d) I and III

37. We need friction for walking. To put a foot forward, we push the other foot backwards on the ground. The friction between our shoe and the ground acts in the opposite direction and prevents our foot from slipping. Thus, we are able to move forward.

In the above diagram, which arrow represents friction acting between the shoe and the ground?

(a) *A* (b) *B* (c) *C* (d) *D*

38. Food preservation ensures that the food lasts for a longer time without getting spoiled. Which of the following methods is used to preserve the food materials?

(a) Drying and dehydration

(b) Sterilisation

(c) Saltation and sweetening

(d) All of the above

39. The animals found in a particular area are termed as fauna of that area. Consider the given animals and select that how many of these are the examples of fauna of Pachmarhi Biosphere Reserve.

A.  B. 

C.  D. 

(a) Only A

(b) Only D

(c) A and D

(d) A, B, C and D

40. **Statement I** The chemical substances produced by microorganisms which in low concentration are antagonistic to the growth of other microorganisms are called as antibiotics.

Statement II A preparation of a dead or attenuated pathogen, which when injected into a healthy person, provides immunity against a number of diseases, is called as vaccine.

Which of the following statement(s) is/are correct?

(a) Only I

(b) Only II

(c) Both I and II

(d) None of the above

2 Marks Questions

41. Lightning can be seen, the moment it occurs. Aditi observes lightning in her area. She hears the sound 5 s after she observed lightning. How far is she from the place, where lightning occurs?
[Speed of sound = 330 m/s]
(a) 1000 m (b) 1550 m
(c) 1650 m (d) 1750 m

42. State [T] for True and [F] for False.
I. Light is visible that is why it make the objects visible.
II. Light sometime travels in straight line and sometime it follows a curved path.
III. Angle of incidence is always equal to angle of reflection.
IV. Kaleidoscope consists of curved lenses.

Codes

	I	II	III	IV
(a)	T	T	F	T
(b)	F	F	T	F
(c)	T	F	T	F
(d)	F	T	T	F

43.

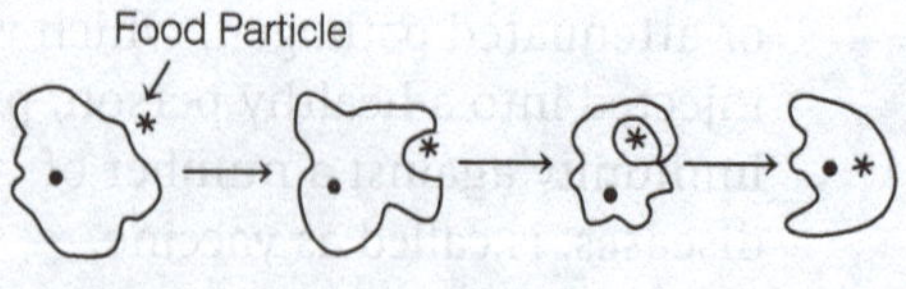

The above diagram shows
(a) endomosis (b) phagocytosis
(c) pinocytosis (d) exocytosis

44. Match the Column I with Column II.

Column I	Column II
A. Master gland	1. Diabetes
B. Male hormone	2. Pituitary gland
C. Insulin	3. Testosterone
D. Female hormone	4. Oestrogen

Codes

	A	B	C	D
(a)	1	2	3	4
(b)	4	3	2	1
(c)	2	3	1	4
(d)	1	2	4	3

45. A person goes through the stages of growth given below. Choose the correct sequence from the codes given below.
1. Foetus 2. Zygote 3. Embryo
4. Baby 5. Adult
6. Adolescent 7. Child

Codes
(a) 2, 3, 1, 4, 7, 6, 5 (b) 2, 1, 3, 4, 7, 5, 6
(c) 3, 2, 1, 4, 6, 7, 5 (d) 1, 3, 2, 4, 7, 6, 5

46. Ram and Vaibhav performed experiments taking similar bulbs and cells but two different solutions A and B shown below.

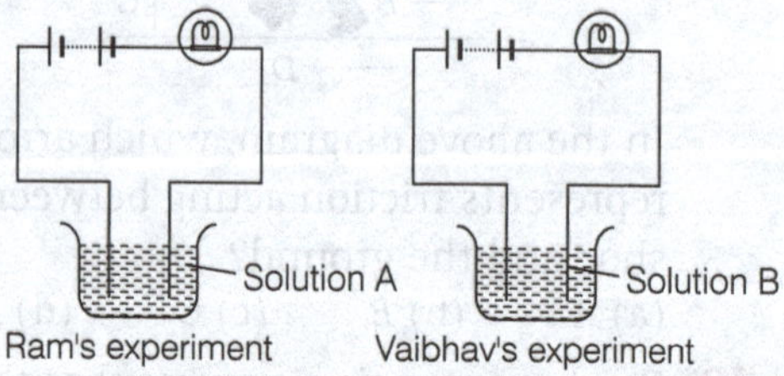

They found that the bulb in the setup A glows more brightly as compared to that of the setup B. You would conclude that
(a) Higher current is flowing through the circuit in setup A.
(b) Higher current is flowing through the circuit in setup B.
(c) Equal current is flowing through both the circuits.
(d) The current flowing through the circuits in the two setups cannot be compared in this manner.

47. Three friends, Salman, Adnan and Farhan argue as follows

Salman CNG is the least polluting fuel for vehicles.

Adnan Lignite is used for surfacing of road.

Farhan Petrol and diesel are the cleanest fuel for vehicles.

Who made the correct statement?

(a) Salman
(b) Adnan
(c) Farhan
(d) Adnan and salman

48. Which of the following statements describes the given microbe correctly?

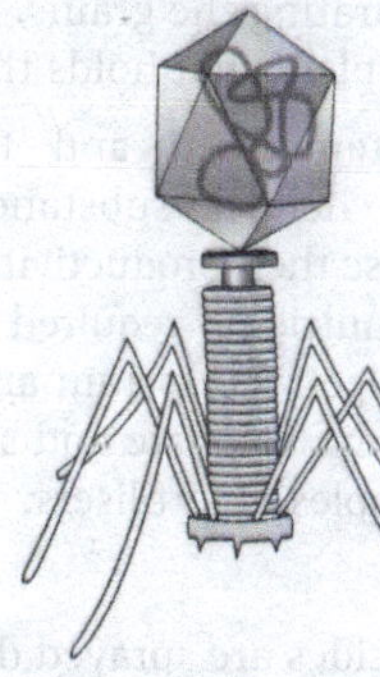

(a) It is a bacterium which causes diseases in plants
(b) It is a type of virus which attacks bacteria
(c) It is a bacterium which kills viruses
(d) It can multiply inside both living and non-living cells

49. The pressure on the tyres of a sedan car is 220 kPa. The contact surface of each tyre with the floor is 200 cm^2. Calculate the new contact surface of each tyre when air is released from the tyre and the pressure of the car is reduced to 180 kPa.

(a) 240 cm^2
(b) 200 cm^2
(c) 245 cm^2
(d) 500 cm^2

50. Identify the incorrect labeling in the given diagram.

$A \rightarrow$ Eye spot
$B \rightarrow$ Nucleus
$C \rightarrow$ Chloroplast
$D \rightarrow$ Flagellum
$E \rightarrow$ Contractile vacuole
$F \rightarrow$ Pyrenoid

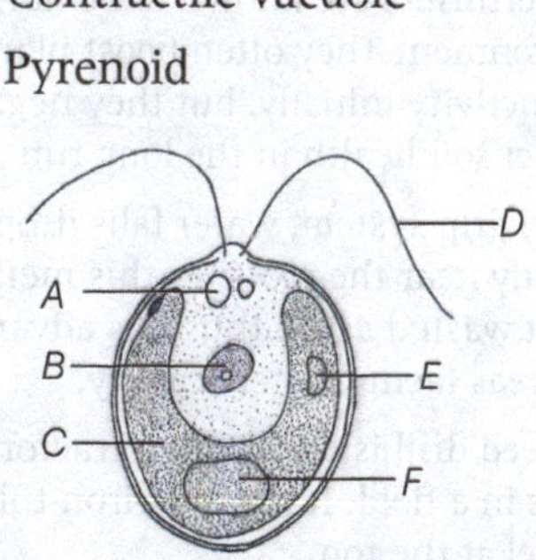

(a) Both A and E
(b) Both C and F
(c) Only D
(d) Only B

Hints & Solutions

Crop Production and Management

1. (*c*) Bean is a legume, not a cereal crop.
2. (*a*) From the given crop list, the Kharif's crop can be grouped as
   Maize, Paddy, Groundnut, Cotton
3. (*b*) The seeds that are of a bad quality will float when kept in water as they are hollow inside because they lack carbohydrates and starch required for seed germination.
4. (*a*) Chemical fertilisers are rich in mineral acids which can increase the acidity in soil.
5. (*b*) *X* is fertiliser containing the chemical elements that improve growth and productivity of plants.
   Y is organic manure that are naturally produced.
6. (*d*) Fertilisers are known to be harmful to environment.They often boost plant productivity initially, but they negatively impact soil health in the long run.
7. (*b*) In drip system, water falls drop by drop directly near the roots. In this method, water is not wasted at all, thus it is advantageous for areas facing water scarcity.
8. (*c*) Seed drill is used with a tractor for sowing seeds in a field. It is a long iron tube having funnel at the top.
9. (*c*) Hoe is a simple tool which is used for removal of weeds and also loosening the soil.
10. (*a*) Ploughing helps in penetration of roots of growing plants. Root penetration ability is critical for plant growth and development.
11. (*a*) The soil is broken down into size of grain to loosen it for mixing nutrients, increase aeration, etc. Plough, hoe and cultivator are used for this process.
12. (*c*) These machinery allow the work to be done faster compared to manual labour. There is a reduction in the dependency on the humans and animals for the work to be done.
13. (*a*) Fungus (*Phytophthora infestans*) causes the blight of potato disease.
14. (*a*) Rice and soyabean are Kharif crops which are sown at the onset of monsoon (July-October). This is because they require good water quantity and depend on rainfall patterns for their growth.
15. (*b*)
16. (*b*) To replenish the nutrients, farmers can add manures, left field uncultivated between two crops or perform crop rotation, i.e. leguminous crops between cereal crops.
    Excessive use of fertilisers can lead to soil acidification.
17. (*b*) Process of loosening and turning the soil is termed as ploughing or tilling. Threshing consist of separating the grains, from the portion of the plant that holds them.
18. (*a*) Both statements I and II are correct. Fertilisers are chemical substances supplied to crops to increase their productivity. They contain the essential nutrients required by the plants, including nitrogen, potassium and phosphorus. Urea, ammonium sulphate and superphosphate are some examples of fertilisers.
19. (*b*)
20. (*b*) The weedicides are sprayed during the vegetative growth of weeds before flowering and seed formation.
21. (*a*) This is a traditional method of irrigation called as dhekli used to draw water from wells, lakes, canals, etc.
22. (*a*) Weedicides are the special chemicals which are sprayed over fields to get rid of weeds but they will not show any effect on crop plants.
23. (*a*) Weeds don't help the plants grow healthily. They grow faster and sucks up the nutrients and minerals from the soil and destroy the main crop of resources.
24. (*c*) The correct identification of labels is
    P—Legumes or pulses.
    Q—Wheat, rice, barley, etc.
    R—Sugarcane or beetroots.
    S—Mustard, sunflower, groundnuts, etc.
25. (*b*)

26. (*a*) A-4, B-2, C-3, D-1. It can be explained as

1. Threshing consists of separating the grains, from the portion of the plant that holds them is done by wing thresher.
2. Hoe is used for tilling the soil. Tilling is the practice of aerating the soil to permit moisture.
3. The function of a combine is to cut, thresh and clean grains.
4. Leveller is used in ploughed soil to prevent soil erosion

27. (*c*)

28. (*b*) I. Apart from good quality seeds, using appropriate agricultural practices are important for getting higher yield.
II. It actually enriches the soil
III. Some crop plants need transplantation
IV. Rhizobium present in the cells of root nodules of leguminous plants fix nitrogen.

29. (*a*)

30. (*b*) Statements I and IV are supports the above claim. It can be explained as
In sprinkler system, the water is allowed to pass through a system of pipes at a high pressure. This allows the nozzles to rotate and sprinkle water covering a large circular area. There is no deposition of water on ground thus, water logging is prevented.

31. (*d*)

32. (*a*) Beans, grams, peas, etc., are leguminous plants. These plants are capable of replenishing the depleted nitrogen levels in soil. These plants have *Rhizobium* living symbiotically within their roots, which is capable of fixing atmospheric N_2 and convert it into simple forms.

33. (*a*) A-2, B-4, C-1, D-3.

Microorganisms : Friend & Foe

1. (*c*) *Rhizobium* is a non-motile, rod-shaped bacteria, while others are of varying shapes and are motile.

2. (*a*) Statements I and II are correct. The correct form of other statements are *Penicillium* is a fungi microorganism while *spirogyra* is an algal microorganism. Protozoa have the ability to move and find their food.

3. (*c*) Influenza, chickenpox, common cold have virus as a causative agent.

4. (*a*) A bacterial cell is enclosed by a cell wall, with cytoplasm and a circular DNA which represents its nuclear material.

5. (*d*) Lichens are symbiotic association between a fungi (which provides shelter) and an algae (which manufactures) food with the help of photosynthesis). It is a mutually beneficial relationship.

6. (*d*) Chlorophyllous refers to the organisms containing chlorophyll, who can perform photosynthesis, e.g. *Chlamydomonas* as shown by figure (D).

7. (*a*)

8. (*c*) *Entamoeba* is a single-celled microbe, identified as a habitat of water bodies like lakes, ponds and rivers. It is found as internal parasite or commensals in the human gastrointestinal tract. They falls under the phylum-Protozoa.

9. (*c*) Foot and mouth diseases is a virus disease in animals.
Anton Van Leeuwenhoek is father of micro biology.
Female *Aedes* mosquito is carrier of dengue.

10. (*b*) The organisms is bread mould, a type of fungus. It reproduces by spores, and is known to spoil the food materials. It absorbs nutrients from host's organism as well as from dead and decaying organism therefore, have both mode of nutrition-saprophytic and parasitic.

11. (*a*)

12. (*a*) Bacteriophage virus has a complex structure. Influenza, adeno and tobacco mosaic virus have spherical, polyhedral and helical shape.

13. (*c*) The statements II and IV are incorrect. The correct form of these statements are Bacterial cells lack a defined nucleus.
Exchanging genetic information is not a method of sexual reproduction.

14. (*b*) Yeast has been used for the large scale production of alcohol or wine. The process of conversion of sugar to alcohol is known as fermentation.

15. (*b*) The presence of food and moisture favours the growth of fungus.

16. (*b*) *Spirogyra* can be used as a source of food. It consists of proteins, lipids, carbohydrates, dietary fibres, etc.

17. (*b*) Female *Anopheles* is carrier of malaria.

18. (*a*) Malaria, filariasis and dengue are caused by female mosquito while typhoid is caused by insect vector flies, i.e. housefly.

19. (*c*) In group C, all diseases are the caused by bacterial pathogens, i.e.
Anthrax—*Bacillus anthracis*
Typhoid—*Salmonella typhi*
Tuberculosis—*Mycobacterium tuberculosis*
Cholera—*Vibrio cholerae*

20. (*b*) A-2, B-3, C-4, D-1

21. (*b*) Organisms like *Nostoc, Rhizobium* and *Anabaena* (helps in nitrogen fixation), *Lactobacillus* (curd formation), *Aspergillus* (secretes penicillin) are identified as beneficial for humans. While *Entamoeba* and *Bacillus anthracis* are pathogens.

22. (*c*) We know that due to food spoiled there are some changes occur such as change in colour of food, change in taste of food, gas formation etc. But there is no change in size of food.

23. (*a*) Some bacteria like *Clostridium* and *Staphylococci* and fungi like *Aspergillus* cause food poisoning. Yeast is used in the production of alcohol.

24. (*b*) An antibiotic is a chemical substance secreted by a bacteria/fungi or other microbes which can kill or prevent the growth of disease causing bacteria.

25. (*b*) Statements II and III are incorrect and can be corrected as
Foot and mouth disease of cattle is caused by a virus.
The bacterium which promotes the formation of curd is *Lactobacillus*.

26. (*d*) Anthrax is an animal disease which is caused by bacteria, i.e. *Bacillus anthracis*.

- Anthrax is not a common disease.
- Louis Pasteur discovered the process of fermentation.
- Jams, jellies and squashes are preserved by sugar.

27. (*c*) Statements III and IV are false. The correct form of these statements are

- Yeast produces CO_2, not CH_4.
- Citrus canker is a bacterial disease transmitted through air.

28. (*b*) The process of conversion of atmospheric N_2 to simple easily usable forms (nitrates) for plants is called as nitrogen-fixation.

29. (*a*) *Rhizobium* lives in a symbiotic relationship with roots of leguminous plants, where it forms root nodules in which nitrogen-fixation takes place.

30. (*d*) A-2, B-5, C-4, D-3, E-1.

31. (*c*) Nitrogen present in atmosphere cannot be used by plants as such.
Thus, conversion of atmospheric N_2 is carried out by different sources such as nitrogen-fixing bacteria, fungi and *Rhizobium* present in soil.
Apart of them, lightning also help in the process of nitrogen fixation.

32. (*c*) Milk contains various types of bacteria which are harmless normally but at higher temperature they multiply rapidly and convert the lactose present in milk into lactic acid. This increases the acidity of milk, causing breakdown of protein and separation of liquid.

33. (*d*) A-3, B-4, C-1, D-2

34. (*d*) *Aspergillus* is a fungal microorganism.

35. (*b*) The correct events are as follows,
At *P*—*Rhizobium* is forming root nodules where nitrogen-fixation occurs.
At *Q*—Nitrogen from air is being fixed.
At *R* and *S*—Nitrification occurs.
At *T*—Denitrification is taking place.

36. (*b*)

Coal and Petroleum

1. (*d*) Coke and charcoal are amorphous allotropes of carbon whereas graphite is its crystalline allotrope. Thus, all these are its free form. Petrol is a mixture of several hydrocarbons (i.e. compounds of carbon and hydrogen).

2. (*c*) Coal tar is a thick, black, opaque fluid obtained as a by-product of the process of manufacturing coke.
3. (*c*) Exhaustible natural resources are limited in nature. They can be exhausted by human activities and are dependent on nature.
4. (*b*) Coke being a good reducing agent is usually used in the extraction of metals. Coal tar is used for synthesising plastics, paints, etc. Coal gas is a good fuel, while coal is the remains of vegetation.
5. (*d*) The calorific value of LPG fuel is 50 kJ/g. All other given sets are correctly matched.
6. (*a*) Carbon dioxide, heat and water are formed as product after complete combustion of methane.
7. (*b*)
8. (*d*) All the given actions help in saving petrol.
9. (*a*) Bitumen is obtained from petroleum. Wildlife is an example of exhaustible natural resource. Bitumen is used for surfacing roads. Carbonisation is a very slow process.
10. (*c*) The given properties match with the coal tar, so this substance should be coal tar.
11. (*a*)
12. (*c*) Coke, coal gas and coal tar are the products of processing of coal while CNG is obtained from drilling for petroleum.
13. (*b*) The given statement indicates that X is the coal gas and from it water gas, producer gas and diamond can be prepared.
14. (*a*) Carbonisation is a very slow process of conversion of dead vegetation into coal. Since, coal is obtained from remains of vegetation, it is also called fossil fuel. A very high temperature and pressure is required for the occurrence of this process.
15. (*b*) Coal tar is used as a starting material for the synthesis of various items like synthetic dyes, drugs, explosives, perfumes, plastics, naphthalene balls (used to repel moths and insects), etc.
16. (*b*) Lignite is a type of coal. It contains around 60% of carbon and is also known as brown coal.
17. (*a*) **Peat** It is a dark brown substance like a soil.
    Lignite It is known as brown coal.
    Bituminous It is a black coloured coal.
18. (*a*) Lignite is also known by the name brown coal and contains about 70% carbon.
    Anthracite is the purest variety of carbon as it contains about 90% carbon.
    Peat is the most impure form and contains only 60% carbon, Bituminous is the most common variety and is associated with 78% carbon.
19. (*a*)
20. (*b*) Coal tar is a mixture of about 200 substances. Coke is the most pure form of carbon. It is a porous black material. Coal is a fossil fuel obtained by carbonisation process and it is used in thermal power plants for generating electricity.
21. (*a*) Energy from water and geothermal energy can be good alternative of coal in power station.
22. (*c*) Coal is made up of carbon along with small amounts of oxygen, sulphur, hydrogen and nitrogen. Its main varieties are peat, lignite, bituminous and anthracite. Among these, anthracite is the hardest and contains 90-95% carbon. Peat is the softest variety.
23. (*a*) Oxygen in air is not an exhaustible natural resource because it is present in unlimited quantity in nature.
24. (*b*) X = Above, Y=Lighter
25. (*d*) Natural gas can be easily transported through pipes, so can be used as a fuel at homes for cooking. It can also be used for power generation. It is stored under high pressure as compressed natural gas (CNG), which is a good fuel for vehicles.
26. (*c*) LPG-Liquefied Petroleum Gas (or petroleum gas in liquefied form). Natural gas can be converted into CNG (compressed natural gas) by applying pressure. Petroleum is also known by the name black gold and paraffin wax is used in making vaseline, candles, ointments, etc.
27. (*b*) The calorific value of petrol is 47. All other statements are correct.

28. (*a*) Diesel, paraffin, CNG. Bitumen and kerosene are the constituents of petroleum but coal tar and coal gas are obtained from coal.

29. (*d*) The correct calorific value is/are
Coal - 25-33
Methane - 55
Diesel - 45
Kerosene - 48

30. (*a*)

31. (*b*) It should have a moderate rate of combustion and should release heat in a controlled manner.

32. (*d*)

33. (*c*) The order of different fractions from top to bottom is

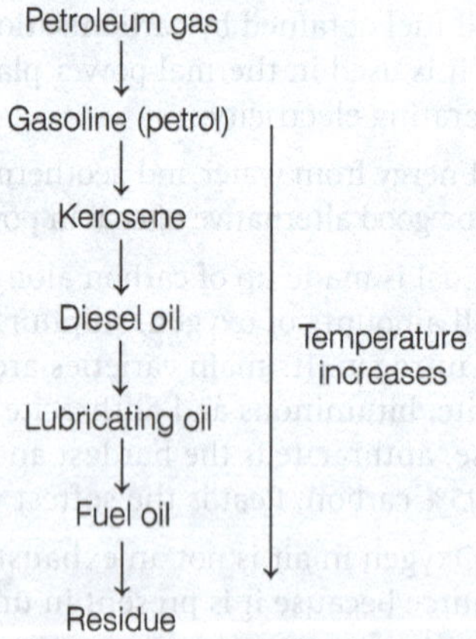

34. (*a*) Natural gas supplied to homes and factories through pipes and is obtained from oil wells. Natural gas is a cleaner fuel and exhaustible source of energy like fossil fuels.

35. (*b*) Anthracite contains around 86% or higher carbon content. All other statements are true.

36. (*b*) Boiling points of different hydrocarbons are different. Petrochemicals are obtained from petroleum and natural gas and are used in the manufacture of detergents, fibres, etc. Paraffin wax is used of making candles, vaseline, polish, etc.

37. (*b*)Kerosene (paraffin oil) lies in between the petrol and diesel oil. This fraction is used as a fuel for stoves, lamps and jet engines.

38. (*a*) X = coal, Y = limited, Z = always

39. (*c*) Coal is obtained by carbonisation process which is a very slow process (i.e. takes thousands of years) and requires very high temperature and pressure. Existence of such conditions in laboratory is not possible, so coal cannot be prepared in the laboratory.

40. (*b*) The petroleum is subjected to fractional distillation to obtain products of various uses. All other statements are true.

41. (*d*) All given statements are correct.

42. (*c*) Fossil fuels should be conserved because they are available only in limited quantity. Resources present in limited quantity are called exhaustible resources.
Burning of coal in insufficient amount of oxygen produces carbon monoxide, not carbon dioxide.

Combustion and Flame

1. (*b*) The necessary conditions for combustion are availability of air/oxygen, fuel and temperature of fuel is more than its ignition temperature.

2. (*c*) From the given materials list, the combustible materials can be grouped as Charcoal, straw, cardboard, paper, candle, wood.

3. (*d*) Combustion reactions are those reactions which take place slowly and given less amount of heat slowly is called slow combustion. i.e. burning of candle, burning of wood, burning of paper.

4. (*d*) In this experiment, it is seen that candle is burn in glass chimney in which sufficient oxygen is present. So, this experiment shows that, oxygen is essential for combustion.

5. (*c*) Due to incomplete combustion of fuel leading to the formation of soot. This soot when accumulates on the vessels blackens them.

6. (*c*) Ignition temperature of sulphur is high enough, so it does not burn in air at room temperature.
During spontaneous combustion, the material suddenly bursts into flame.
All other given statements are true.

7. (*d*) I. Magnesium is a combustible metal.

II. Calorific value of coal is higher than that of wood.

III. A chemical process in which a substance reacts with oxygen to give off heat is called combustion.

IV. Carbon dioxide is the best extinguisher for fires involving electrical equipment.

8. (*c*) Carbon monoxide is a particles of unburnt carbon (X) added to the environment which leads to respiratory and nervous diseases (Y).

9. (*d*) Oil is lighter than water. So, when it is poured on oil fire, it sinks to the bottom where it evaporates due to the heat of the fire.

10. (*c*) Burning of candle is an example of slow combustion, burning of phosphorus is example of spontaneous reaction (combustion), burning of LPG is an example of rapid combustion and burning of crackers is an example of explosion.

11. (*c*) By covering with a blanket, it prevents the supply of oxygen, which is a supporter of combustion.

12. (*a*)

13. (*d*) When hole is open, oxygen is in excess, so complete combustion takes place and the colour of the flame is blue. When the hole is closed, oxygen supply is not sufficient for the complete combustion of the fuel. Due to incomplete combustion of the fuel, the colour of the flame is yellow.

14. (*d*) When a candle burns, the flame heats the nearby air and this warm air moves up towards lower pressure.

15. (*d*) Energy is largest in non-luminous zone. Outermost zone is the hottest part of the flame. Some fuels burn with flame while some are not.

16. (*a*) I. Charcoal does not vapourise and so does not produce a flame.

II. A blue coloured flame which produces very little light is called non-luminous flame.

III. Goldsmith uses the outer zone of a candle flame because it is the hottest zone.

17. (*c*) Dark zone is the coldest zone, so it takes highest time as compared to two other zones to reach at 50°C.

18. (*a*) For a good fuel, ignition temperature should be low but calorific value should be high.

19. (*b*) Smoke causes respiratory problems, carbon monoxide chocks the throat, oxides of nitrogen causes lung diseases and dust causes allergic reaction.

20. (*c*)

21. (*c*) Total mass of fuel = 4.5 kg

Total heat produced = 180000 kJ

Heat produced by burning 1 kg of fuel

$$= \frac{180000}{4.5} \text{ kJ/kg}$$

$$= 40000 \text{ kJ/kg}$$

22. (*a*)

Fuel	**Calorific value** (kJ/kg)
Wood	17000-22000
Charcoal	25000-33000
Petrol	45000
LPG	55000

23. (*c*) Increased concentration of carbon dioxide in the environment result in increased temperature of the Earth, which is known by the name global warming.

24. (*a*)

25. (*a*) When wood burns, the carbon present in it is oxidised to carbon dioxide, which is a non-poisonous gas. When the windows are closed, the air or oxygen cannot enter the room.

Incomplete supply of oxygen carbon is oxidised to carbon monoxide which is highly poisonous.On opening the windows the poisonous gas slowly diffused out the room and fresh air came inside.

26. (*d*)

27. (*b*) Ignition temperature of A (hydrogen) is very low because of which it catches fire immediately and hence, cannot be considered as an ideal fuel.

28. (*a*)

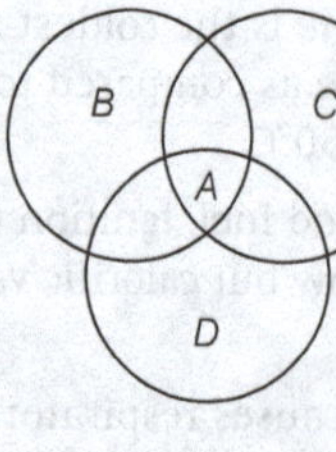

A—Natural fuels, *B*—Wood
C—Coal, *D*—Cowdung cake

29. (*c*) Petrol and diesel on burning produces black smoke with many harmful gases which causes pollution. CNG does not produce any poisonous gases. Hence, it does not cause air pollution. The maintenance of LPG car will always be higher than that of petrol car.

30. (*a*) The watch glass containing petrol will catch fire instantly because its ignition temperature is very low. Also petrol is an inflammable substance, i.e. it can easily catch fire with a flame.

31. (*b*) LPG is highly flammable mixture of these hydrocarbon gases which is used in cooking. Iron nails do not burn on being exposed to flame. Such substances are non-combustible. Candle vaporises while burning produces the flame. Deforestation is the purposeful clearing forested land. Wood is important as a fuel source, building material.

32. (*c*) When fuel is burnt, oxides of sulphur and nitrogen are produced. These oxides when dissolve in rainwater, makes it acidic. Such rain is called acid rain.

33. (*b*) I. Magnesium is a combustible substance because it burns with a intense light and forms ash.

II. Combustion is a chemical process in which a substance reacts rapidly with oxygen and given off heat. All other given statements are true.

34. (*a*) I. Increased in carbon dioxide gas in air is the cause of global warming.

II. A good fuel has a low ignition temperature, produces large amount of heat.

III. CNG is way better fuel than any other fuel. It has no smoke and does not produce any harmful gas.

IV. Kerosene is a clear, flammable liquid distilled from petroleum.

35. (*b*) If change *A* is a chemical change, then, *B* must be a physical change which is reversible in nature.

36. (*a*)

37. (*b*) In rapid combustion, material burns rapidly to give heat and light. During explosion, sound is also produced along with heat and light. Baking soda is a fire extinguisher as it produces CO_2 gas on burning.

In case of spontaneous combustion, the material burns without any apparent cause.

Conservation of Plants and Animals

1. (*d*) The animals who are very few in numbers and thus on verge of being extinct are labelled as critically endangered in Red Data Book.

2. (*b*) Kaziranga National Park in Assam is protected area where conservation projects for one horned rhinoceros are under going.

3. (*b*) The tiger is not an extinct species because living members of this species are still present.

4. (*b*)

5. (*b*) This picture is of a flightless bird called Dodo, that was endemic to island of Mauritius. Since there is no living member of this species on Earth, hence it is now extinct.

6. (*b*) Deforestation impacts all parts of the Earth. It results in reduction of groundwater level, atmospheric moisture, rainfall pattern, etc. The level of CO_2 will rise along with other pollutants. This will lead to increased greenhouse effect and global warming.

7. (*c*) *P* is man made place called zoos, while *Q* is conservation of wild animals in their natural habitats, i.e. wildlife sanctuary.

8. (*a*) Endemic species are those species of plants and animals which are found exclusively in particular area. They often threatened due to introduction exotic species from some other geographical area.

9. (*b*) All the given strategies can be adapted to save our environment, except IV. Keeping birds and animals in our house is not a feasible action.

10. (*c*) Deforestation is cutting down of forests for human requirements. This results in disturbed water cycle which affects rainfall, decrease in groundwater levels, increase in floods and droughts.

11. (*b*) Birds who fly distance to reach another land to avoid inhospitable weather conditions of their habitats are called migratory birds. Siberian crane fly for laying eggs as the weather is their natural habitat becomes very cold and inhospitable.

12. (*a*)

13. (*b*) Deforestation removes the trees which hold the soil together by their roots. Removing the trees leaves the soil bare to wind and other elements which lead to soil erosion due to lack of humus and fertility of soil. This ultimately lead to desertification.

14. (*d*) Dianosours became extinct due to large scale climatic change which eliminated most of the life from the Earth. Food chain imbalances lead to the starvation of the dinosaurs.

Reproduction in Animals

1. (*d*) *B* is the uterus where a fertilised egg undergoes development to form a baby.

2. (*d*) Mature sperm travel through vas deferens from testes and then forwarded to urethra after adding secretion from semniferous tubules and passes into penis.

3. (*a*) A male foetus is formed when *X* and *Y* chromosomes pair up from mother and father, respectively while a foetus is female when *X* and *X* chromosomes pair up from mother and father, respectively

4. (*a*) Animal *X* is starfish. This method is called as external fertilisation where fusion of gametes take place outside of a female body.

5. (*c*) *X*–Ova, *Y*–Sperm and *Z*-Zygote. Ova is a female reproductive cell which fuse with the male reproductive cell-sperm to form zygote.

6. (*a*)

7. (*a*) Only statement (a) is true. The correct form of other statements are
   - Young ones do not necessarily look the same to parents who undergo metamorphosis.
   - Life cycle of silkworm involves → egg → caterpillar → pupa → adult.
   - A tadpole lives in water as they have gills whereas frog can live on land and in water because lungs replace to the gills.

8. (*b*) The organisms is *Hydra* in which asexual reproduction occurs through budding.

9. (*c*) In figure *A*, binary fission in *Amoeba* and in *B*, budding in yeast is depicted. Both these are the methods of asexual reproduction.

10. (*c*) At stage *D*, cytokinesis, i.e. the division of cytoplasm equally among daughter cells takes place.

11. (*b*) Regeneration is the ability of some organisms to form new individuals from their body parts, e.g *Planaria* and starfish show regeneration. Whereas *Amoeba* does not regenerate.

12. (*a*) Both A and R are true, and R is the correct explanation of A. Cloning helps in preserving parental features because the genetic material from parents is copied and propagated asexually.

13. (*c*) In the animals who exhibit viviparity, i.e. which produce young ones, the process of fertilisation, growth and development of embryo to foetus occurs inside female parent's body.

14. (*d*) Statements I, II and IV are incorrect. The correct form of these statements are
   - Human females are viviparous as they give birth to young ones.
   - An egg is fertilised by only one sperm.
   - After 9 months of development in mother's uterus, the baby gets ready for delivery.

15. (*b*) Statements II and IV are incorrect. The correct form of these statements are
   - The animals that lay eggs are known as oviparous animals.
   - Snakes exhibits internal fertilisation, i.e. fusion of gametes take place inside the animal's body.

16. (*c*) Statements I and III are false. The correct form of these statements are
- Fertilisation is not a necessary event is asexual reproduction
- Clones are produced by asexual reproduction.

Age of Adolescence

1. (*c*) The larynx grows larger in size during the puberty. It protrudes out at the front of the throat especially in boys.

2. (*b*) Oestrogen is the female hormone whose production starts when girls reach puberty. It is secreted by ovary and is responsible for appearance of secondary sexual characters in females.

3. (*c*) The appearance of hair in the armpits and pubic area is a common changes at puberty in both the male and female sexes.

4. (*a*) Puberty begin at the age of 12-14 years in males and at 10-13 years in female. This phase is of rapid growth and development.

5. (*d*) The first menstrual period is called menarche. It marks the beginning of a woman's reproductive cycle. Menopause is a natural biological process in which the menstrual cycle stops. It marks the end of a woman's reproductive cycle.

6. (*b*)

7. (*a*) Adolescents grow at a faster rate and thus require proper, healthy diet. This diet gives sufficient nutrients, which are used in growth of the body.

8. (*c*) The insulin hormone is known to lower the blood sugar level. Thus, the doctor has prescribed insulin injection to this patient because he has high blood sugar level.

9. (*d*) Iodine is essential for proper functioning of thyroid gland.

10. (*d*) Trypsin is the odd one out because it is an enzyme, while others are hormones.

11. (*c*) Adrenaline hormone prepares the body for a fight or flight response. In preparation for it, our heartbeat, breathing rate, blood pressure and glucose metabolism increases. Thus, option (c) is correct.

12. (*b*) I depicts the effect of adrenaline secreted from adrenal glands (*G*), while II represents the effects of insulin secreted from pancreas (*H*).

13. (*c*) The figure is showing the condition called goitre. It develops due to deficiency of thyroxine hormone (which requires iodine for its production). Due to this, the thyroid gland enlarges and neck swells too much.

14. (*a*) Gland *X* is the pituitary which secretes the growth hormone. The secretion of less hormone results in dwarfism in which body does not grow and person remains very short while excess hormone results in gigantism, i.e. body grows extremely tall.

15. (*a*) *X* represents the process of fertilisation, i.e. the fusion of male and female gametes. If it happens then the zygote divides to form embryo which gets implanted in uterine wall and establish pregnancy. In absence of fertilisation, the uterine line is shed as menstrual bleeding.

16. (*a*) Endocrine glands secrete hormones directly into the bloodstream from where they reach the target site, e.g. pituitary, adrenal and thymus gland.
Exocrine gland secretes substances onto an epithelial surface using a duct, e.g.—sweat, salivary, prostate gland, etc. Liver and pancreas have both exocrine and endocrine functions.

17. (*a*) Part labelled *P*-*S* are correctly identified as
- *P*—Ovary, site of gamete production.
- *Q*—Fallopian tube, site of fertilisation.
- *R*—Uterus, site of development of embryo.
- *S*—Vagina, passage for entry of sperms.

Force and Pressure

1. (*d*) A force is a push or a pull which can change the state of rest or motion of an object. It can change direction of motion.
A force can also change the speed of a moving object.

2. (*d*) Friction opposes the state of an object. The force needed to push the box is least for *D*. Therefore, friction will also be least for *D*.

3. (*a*) Magnitude of force applied by Ram is greater than that of Shyam because only the displacement will be towards Shyam.

4. (*b*) Attractive magnetic force acts between the electromagnets and the metallic hammer which makes the hammer strike the gong.

5. (*d*)

6. (*d*) The deep treads on the tyre are to increase friction. As rough surface has more friction. Thus, it reduces the chance of slipping.

7. (*a*) Statements I, II and IV are false and can be corrected as

I. Not only by the Earth there are also other heavenly bodies which exert gravitational force.

II. Force between two electric charges is called electrostatic forces.

IV. Muscular and frictional forces are the examples of contact forces.

8. (*b*) Gravitational force and magnetic force extend the spring, whereas elastic force tries to move the spring back.

9. (*a*) Statement IV is false and can be corrected as IV force between two charged bodies is called electrostatic force.

10. (*c*) This happens when the force exerted by the opposite teams are equal.

11. (*c*) Friction is a force and unit of force is newton (N).
Weight = mg = Force.
This implies that weight is also a force.
So, unit of weight is also in newton (N).

12. (*b*) The main force acting on parachute is gravity when you first release the parachute, the force of gravity pulls it downward, and the parachute speeds toward the ground.

13. (*d*) When the girl tries to walk, she pushes the ground backward due to which the ground provides a frictional force to the feet in the forward direction, i.e. in the direction of walking (D).

14. (*b*) The spring B is compressed most as compared to the other springs due to the greater weight of woman at this point of chair.

15. (*c*) The effect of the force depends on the magnitude of force and the area of surface on which it is applied. The effect of force takes place in the direction of the force applied.

16. (*d*) The object does not fall as the tension in the string acts against the weight or Earth's gravity.

17. (*b*) Match II and III are correct, but I and IV are incorrect. The incorrect match can be corrected as
In case I, the button on the top of pen is pushed while in case IV, the object placed on the book is pulled upward.

18. (*b*)

19. (*c*) As, pressure is given by, $p = F / A$ thus, increasing area of contact reduces the pressure on their heads.

20. (*d*) The lorry least likely to sink is the one which exerts the smallest pressure on the soft ground.
Since, pressure = $\frac{\text{force}}{\text{area}}$
So, the lorry least likely to sink has the smallest weight and the largest number of wheels, i.e. an empty lorry with six wheels.

21. (*b*) In two rods, which rod her less thickness will sink first. Y will sink first because it has less surface area so it will exert more pressure on sand than the thicker rod X.

22. (*a*) As, B and C have same vertical depth. Thus, pressure on both the points (which is equal to height × density of water) will be same and thus, water will flow out at same pressure from these taps.

23. (*b*) Pressure at depth due to liquid column depends upon height of liquid. So, the order of pressure exerted by the fluid. P, Q, R and S at the bare is given by

$$p_S > p_Q > p_P > p_R$$

24. (*a*) The pressure will be maximum for position A as area of contact is least in Fig. (A) and pressure = force/area.

25. (*c*) Water exerts pressure in all directions at any given depth.
Therefore, it exerts pressure on the wall as on the bottom of the bucket.
Hence, both statements are correct.

26. (*a*) The pressure at a depth l below the water surface is given by

$$P(l) = P_0 + \rho g l$$

Due to this increase in pressure with increasing depth and the thickness of wall increases to stabilise the dam.

27. (*c*) The air molecules inside a balloon collides and create a large pressure on the boundary of balloon, thus increasing its size.

28. (*d*) The pressure exerted by a liquid depends on the vertical depth of the liquid. From the diagram, the water level in each container has the same vertical height. So, the pressure exerted will be same in each vessel.

29. (*d*) Pressure increases with the increase in depth. Thus, pressure at $A <$ pressure at $B <$ pressure at C.

30. (*a*) Statement IV is false and can be corrected as In 'Tug of War', when both the teams apply equal pulling forces, then the net force is zero. All other statements are true.

31. (*c*) Pressure, $p = \dfrac{\text{force}}{\text{area}}$

Here, force = weight = 80 N

and area = area of contact with ground $= 10 \times 5 \text{ cm}^2$

$$\therefore \quad p = \frac{80}{10 \times 5} \text{ N/cm}^2$$

32. (*b*) To suck juice through a pipe, create a partial vacuum.

Juice rises through the pipe until the pressure in the pipe at the juice level equals atmospheric pressure.

33. (*c*) When pressure is applied on a closed liquid container, then it is transmitted equally in all the directions inside it.

34. (*c*) Statements I, III and IV are incorrect and can be corrected as

I. The ratio of force to area always defines the pressure.

III. For a given depth the liquid exerts the same pressure in all directions according to Pascal's law.

IV. Liquid particles have rapid motion and continuously colliding with each other and with the wall of the container.

35. (*c*) As the paper clip move along the ramp, frictional force work between the ramp and the clip, magnetic force attracts the paper clip and gravitational force is trying to keep the paper clip down.

36. (*d*)

37. (*a*) Friction is acting in all the three cases. In cases I and II, air friction acts on objects while in case III, the frictional force due to brakes slow down the bicycle.

38. (*b*)

39. (*a*) A-4, B-3, C-1, D-2.

It can be explained as

A running child applies force with the help of his muscles and this makes him run faster. The air molecules applies force (force = pressure × area) on the walls of the balloons which inflates the balloon.

A woman applies force by her muscles and moves a stationary object. A cricketer applies the force in the opposite direction of the movement of ball and stops it.

40. (*c*)

41. (*b*) The force of gravity is same for all tubes as they are identical and have same amount of toothpaste initially.

As more amount of toothpaste is accumulated on plate below tube 1 than that below tube 3, so more force is applied on tube 1 and more amount of toothpaste is left in tube 3.

42. (*b*) Pressure is the force applied on a unit area of contact and is given by, $p = F/A$

Its SI unit is pascal or Pa.

Hence, only statement B is incorrect.

Friction

1. (*c*) When the box is moved across the floor, frictional force comes into play. It acts in opposite direction to the motion of the box and makes the box to stop.

2. (*a*) The direction of friction is always opposite the direction of motion. Force D is the action force that the shoe exerts on the ground. The reaction force, i.e. the friction acting on the shoe opposes the force D and hence acts in the direction of A.

3. (*b*) The direction of friction *F* always opposes the direction of the pulling force *P*.
The weight of object '*w*' always acts vertically downwards from the centre of gravity of the object.

4. (*c*) The road applies a friction force whenever a car is moving or at rest. When brakes are applied the friction of the road will help the car to stop. The greater the friction the lesser time it will require to stop the car. Hence, the smaller distance will be covered.

5. (*c*) She is least likely to slip on bricks as it will provide maximum friction to her due to its rough surface.

6. (*d*) The force of friction acts between two surfaces irrespective of whether the object is solid, liquid or gaseous.

7. (*b*) Friction acts in opposite direction to the motion of object. Moreover, it acts between the surfaces. Thus, the force of friction in the given case will act on the box from left to right (→).

8. (*a*) Friction will be maximum at *P* as it is most rough.

9. (*c*) Friction always opposes the applied force. So, the force must be applied in the direction of *R*.

10. (*a*) As the roughness of surface increases the friction increases. Hence, the correct order of increasing force of friction is
wet marble floor < dry marble floor < newspaper < towel.

11. (*c*) Frictional force is the opposing force acting in case of ball moving. This cause, the ball to stop after a while.

12. (*a*) Maximum distance is covered on the surface having least friction. Among given surfaces, icy surface has least friction. So, stone cover maximum distance on icy surface.

13. (*b*) Lubricating hinge of door with oil decreases friction and hence, movement of door becomes smooth.

14. (*c*) To reduce friction, boy should spread talcum on the wooden surface. A thin layer is formed over the surfaces in contact and they do not directly rub against each other. Interlocking of irregularities is avoided to a great extent and hence, movement becomes smooth.

15. (*c*) Sliding friction is smaller than static friction. Rolling fricting is still smaller than the sliding friction.
Hence, the correct order is
Static friction > sliding friction > rolling friction.

16. (*a*) Static friction is greater than sliding friction. It is more difficult to bring a body into motion from the rest than to keep a body moving.

17. (*b*) Rocket, bird, etc., have streamlined shape to reduce the area of contact with air and hence to reduce air friction.

18. (*c*) Frictional force acts in opposite direction to that of the motion, i.e. in direction *S*.

19. (*a*) Rollers reduce the friction in roller-skates.

20. (*b*) Friction can be reduced by using rollers, lubricants, ball bearing, etc.

21. (*a*) As the object is at rest, so static friction acts on it. Static friction always becomes equal to the applied force until body starts moving. Hence, when the applied force is doubled, then friction is also doubled.

22. (*c*) Lubricants, streamlined bodies, polished surface and ball bearing reduce friction. However, heat does not reduce friction. But friction can produce heat.

23. (*d*) Friction is more on a dry floor than a wet floor.

24. (*d*) As rolling friction is much less than that of static friction between two surfaces in contact, so its value must be less than 20 N.

25. (*b*) Friction acts on an object opposite to the direction of its motion irrespective of whether it is moving or not.

26. (*b*) Without friction we can't live happily because all the objects are moving due to friction.
Also, if we move by any kind of external force, then we can't stop ourselves, if friction is not present in nature. So, the life will not be easy.

27. (*c*) Friction occurs because most surfaces are not smooth. Friction opposes motion.

28. (*c*) I. The force of friction is independent of the area of the surfaces in contact.
II. Friction opposes motion.
IV. Solids and liquids do not allow things to move over in them, without any external force.
Thus, correct statement is III.

29. (*d*)

30. (*a*) Rough surfaces provide more friction. Wheels decreases the area of contact between the tyre and surface and hence, reduces the friction. Submarines and rockets have streamlined bodies to reduce air friction. In space or vacuum, there is no friction.

Sound

1. (*c*) In a whistle, the air column vibrates to produce sound.

2. (*c*) This type of instrument is called jal tarang.

3. (*c*) Sound waves are material waves, i.e. they need a medium for their propagation. Sound waves cannot travel in vacuum.
So, sound could not be heard in given case.

4. (*b*) Sound needs a medium to propagate. So, it will travel in all given media except vacuum.

5. (*a*) The sound travel fastest in the medium having highest density. As steel has highest density among all hence, sound travel fastest in steel.

6. (*c*) More the air-column, more is the vibration. Hence, the intensity of sound will be maximum in the jar filled less than half.

7. (*a*) More the air column, more is the vibration hence, more will be the sound.

8. (*d*) Solids are packed together tighter than liquids and gases, hence sound travels fastest in solids and slowest in liquid and gases.

9. (*d*) Sound waves require a medium in order to be transmitted. In a glass jar with no air, there is a vacuum which cannot transmit sound.
Similarly, in outer space, there is also a vacuum which cannot transmit sound.

10. (*b*) Speed of sound is fastest in a solid, slower in a liquid and slowest in a gas.
So, given order is air < water < steel.

11. (*a*) As sound travels faster in solids. So, the person is able to hear an approaching train.

12. (*c*) Except tabla and piano, all are string based instruments.

13. (*c*) Sound requires a material medium for its propagation, while light does not.

14. (*c*) Sound needs a medium for propagation, hence sound cannot travel through a vaccum as there are no particles present for vibrations to take place.

15. (*d*) Sound needs a medium to travel, it cannot propagate in vaccum.
A medium can be air, water, metal or anything.

16. (*d*)

17. (*d*) Eustachian tube does not vibrate itself. It carries the sensation of vibration of sound from inner ear to brain.

18. (*b*) The tartar is removed by a scalar, having a hook at its one end.

19. (*c*)

20. (*a*) Range of audible human sound frequency is 20 Hz (or 0.02 kHz) to 20000 Hz (or 20 kHz).
Hence, 100 kHz is above the normal audible range.

21. (*b*) The middle part of the ear amplifies the sound and it consists of three bones hammer, anvil and stirrup.

22. (*a*) Sound waves with frequencies less than 20 Hz are called infrasonic waves.

23. (*c*)

24. (*c*) Total time = 20 s, speed = 1.5 km s^{-1}

$$\therefore \text{Depth of the sea, } d = \frac{\text{speed} \times \text{total time}}{2}$$

$$= \frac{1.5 \times 20}{2} = 15 \text{ km}$$

25. (*c*) The frequencies determine the pitch of a sound and the amplitude determine the loudness.
Noise is the irregular vibration, while music is the regular vibration.

26. (*c*) Statements I and III are true, but statements II and IV are false and can be corrected as

II. Only sound requires a medium for propagation, light can propagate in vaccum also.

IV. The pitch of the sound is affected by the frequency of sound while loudness is affected by the amplitude.

27. (*b*) The pitch of a sound depends directly on the frequency. Higher the frequency higher will be the pitch.

Thus, sound produced by bees which are not carrying honey has a higher pitch.

28. (*c*) Image III has higher frequency than image I as III represents the more number of oscillations.

29. (*c*) Higher the frequency, higher the pitch and higher the shrillness of sound and *vice-versa*. So, IV and V are odd.

30. (*c*)

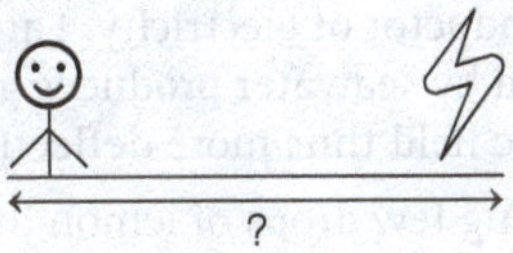

$$\text{Speed} = \frac{\text{distance}}{\text{time}}$$

Distance = speed × time

$= 330 \times 10$ s

$= 3300$ m

31. (*b*) Distance = speed × time

$= 330 \times 5$

$= 1650$ m

$= 1.65$ km

32. (*a*) $\text{Frequency} = \frac{\text{No. of oscillation}}{\text{Time}}$

$= \frac{40}{20} = 2$ Hz

33. (*d*) Given, $f = 500$ vibrations $= 500$ Hz

Time-period, $T = \frac{1}{500} = 0.002$ s

34. (*a*) The loudness and pitch of sound depends on amplitude and frequency of the sound wave, respectively.

So, for louder note of higher pitch, the amplitude and frequency will be larger than the first.

35. (*c*) Both are correct statements. To minimise the noise pollution in residential area individual should keep these points in mind.

I. TV and all music system should play at low volumes.

II. The noisy operations should be conducted away from residential area.

36. (*b*) When Ram stuck the drum with stick, the drum will vibrate, but sounds needs a medium for propagation. So, in vaccum, Ram can not hear the sound of vibrations.

37. (*d*) Statements I and IV are true, but statements II and III are false and can be corrected as

II. Sound requires a medium to travel but light can travel in vacuum.

III. Sound propagates in all directions.

38. (*b*) Statements I and III are correct, other statement are incorrect and can be corrected as

II. Sound higher than 20000 Hz is called ultrasonic.

IV. Ultrasonic waves are used to measure the depth of a sea.

39. (*c*) Ultrasonic sound are audible to bat but not audible to man, it has frequency more than 20 kHz and infrasonic sound have frequency below 20 Hz, i.e. below the lower range of audible frequency. These can be heard by rhinoceros.

40. (*b*) Statements II and III are incorrect and can be corrected as

II. Sudden exposure to high noise can cause a hearing impairment.

III. Use of amplifiers and loudspeakers should be restricted.

41. (*a*)

42. (*d*) Statements III and IV are true, but Statements I and II are false can be corrected as

I. Ultrasonic waves are used to kill bacteria in liquids.

II. Infrasonic waves are produced by the vibration of the Earth's surface during the earthquake.

43. (*d*) The middle part of the ear amplifies the sound and is represented by *C* in the figure which consists of three bones- hammer, anvil and stirrup.

Chemical Effects of Electric Current

1. (*d*) Sodium ions are positively charged, so they are attracted towards negative electrode. Similar is the case with chlorine ions.

2. (*b*) When current is passed through copper sulphate, it dissociates into copper and sulphate ions. This free copper ion deposits on one of the electrode.

3. (*b*) Milk, honey and glass are bad conductors of electricity, whereas water with impurities is a good conductor of electricity and pure water is bad conductor.

4. (*c*) Saline water is a good conductor of electricity. So, scientist must add salt to it.

5. (*a*) An electrochemical cell, the electrode connected to positive terminal of a battery is called anode and that connected to the negative terminal is called cathode.

6. (*b*) Conduction tester is used determine whether a substance is a good or poor conductor of electricity.

7. (*c*) Non-metals are poor conductors of electricity as they do not have conduction electrons.

8. (*d*)

9. (*d*) An electric current can produce chemical, heating and magnetic effects.

10. (*a*) The change in colour of the solution is due to the chemical effect of current.

11. (*d*) An electrolyte should be able to dissociate into ions (positive and negative) so that the ions can move and lead to current.

12. (*b*) During electrolysis of water, water dissociates into positive hydrogen ions and negative oxygen ions. The positive hydrogen ions are attracted by the negative electrode which is C_2.

13. (*d*) Distilled water is a bad conductor of electricity. Sugar solution also does not conduct electricity very well.

14. (*c*) As, the ends of metallic wire are not connected to the battery, so the circuit is not closed and no current flows in the circuit. Then, electrons move in random directions, so that the resultant effect will be zero.

15. (*a*) This process release electrons in potato. When these electrons move from negative to positive terminal of electrode, it reacts with a part of wire inside potato and makes a complex which is green in colour.

16. (*b*) Metallic ions are positive ions which get deposited on cathode.

17. (*d*)

18. (*d*) Sodium chloride, copper sulphate and silver nitrate are good electrolytes whereas sugar solution is a bad conductor of electricity.

19. (*d*) Sugar solution, distilled water and honey does not produce electricity because of zero or low presence of salts which can produce ions.

20. (*d*) Seawater is very salty and salt solution is a good conductor of electricity. Larger current produced by seawater produces greater magnetic field thus more deflection.

21. (*a*) Adding few drops of lemon juice in water will increase the conductivity of solution. The current flow in both cases, but adding of lemon juice makes easy the current to flow.

22. (*a*)

23. (*a*) The water used by fireman to douse fire is ordinary water that contains minerals and impurities. So, it is a good conductor of electricity.

Hence, to prevent electrocution, they shut off electricity supply.

24. (*d*) The flow of electric current through a conducting solution causes chemical reactions. Change in colour of solution may occur deposition of metal may be seen on electrodes. Bubbles may be seen hear the electrodes.

25. (*a*) LED's consumes much lower electricity. So, they are economical. Also, they are available in many colours. LED has applications in many purposes. Ordinary bulb can glow only when the current supply is sufficient to give its wattage value.

26. (*a*) In an LED, the longer terminal is always connected to positive terminal of battery and shorter terminal is connected to negative terminal of the cell.

27. (*c*) Silver, gold and chromium are used for electroplating.

28. (*b*) Statements I and III are correct. Other statements are incorrect and can be corrected as

II. Electroplating means deposition of a layer of desired metal over other with electricity.

IV. Chromium is a metal which does not corrode is resistant from scratches and has a shiny appearance.

29. (*d*) Conduction tester is used to find the conductivity of material whether it is good or bad conductor.

Iron fillings do not form continuous conducting path, so they can't be used in conduction tester.

30. (*d*) In the electroplating factories, the disposal of the used conducting solution is a major concern. It is a polluting waste and there are specific disposal guidelines to protect the environment.

31. (*c*) The current through a circuit is too weak, we can use LED because it glows even when a small electric current flows through it.

32. (*b*) It can be explained as

CFL has a very small amount of mercury (about 4g) sealed inside. LED are much cheaper and cost efficient than CFL. An electric circuit is a closed conducting path in which an electric current flows. Milk is a bad conductor of electricity.

33. (*b*) Statements I and IV are true and statements II and IV are false statement can be corrected as

II. The object to be electroplated during electroplating is always made cathode

III. Chemical effect of electric current is used for the conduction of electricity through the solution.

34. (*b*)II. All wires used in electric circuits should be covered with non-conducting material.

III. Heating effect of the current is responsible for the glow of bulb in an electric circuit.

V. Anode is positive electrode.

35. (*d*) I. Addition of salt makes the distilled water more conducting.

II. During the electrolysis of water, hydrogen gas is liberated at the cathode.

36. (*c*)

Insulator	→ Distilled water
Conductor	→ Sea water
Electrolyte in lemon juice	→ Citric acid
Non-metal	→ Poor conductor

37. (*a*)

38. (*b*)

39. (*d*) Metals are more conducting than the electrolyte. It is because solid metals have excess electrons on surface and hence better conductor than liquid.

40. (*b*)

Some Natural Phenomenon

1. (*b*) A lightning conductor is a device used to protect buildings from the damaging effects of the lightning. If lightning strikes the building, the lightning conductor provides an easy path for the lightning bolt to pass through the ground.

2. (*a*) When storm clouds are developed during thunderstorm, strong wind move upwards and the clouds rub against each other. Due to this friction charges are developed in the clouds.

The upper layers of clouds get positively changed and the lower layers get negatively charged.

3. (*c*)

4. (*d*) The top of the cloud becomes positively charged while the base of the cloud becomes positively charged. Thus, both charges are stored in clouds.

5. (*b*) The pointed end of umbrella may attract lightning, so an umbrella should be avoided during lightning and thunder.

6. (*d*) If one is travelling by a car during lightning, he is safe inside the car with windows and doors of car shut. Because metallic body of a car prevents lighthing to hit a person inside.
The lightning gets discharged to the ground by metallic frame of the car.

7. (*c*) Ozone gas is formed in air during lightning that absorbs ultraviolet radiation present in the sunlight.

8. (*a*) The clothes are rubbed against each other and thus static charge is developed between the clothes.

9. (*a*) It is because light travels much faster than sound. Speed of light is 3×10^8 ms^{-1} and speed of sound is 342 ms^{-1}.

10. (*a*) Mobile phones and cordless phones do not have a conducting path for lightning as landline phones have. This makes them safer to use during lightning or thunderstorm.

11. (*a*) Lightning conductor can protect buildings from the effect of lightning.
One end of the lightning rod is kept out in the air and other is kept burried in the ground. Electrical lights must be unplugged during a thunderstorm.

12. (*d*) A seismograph is the instrument that is used to detect an earthquake. It consists of a seismometer, which may be a pendulum mounted on a spring.

13. (*d*) Lightning is just a strong electric discharge, so it cannot cause tsunami.

14. (*a*) The earthquake is caused by the disturbance deep down inside the uppermost layer of the earth called the crust.

15. (*a*) Earthquake is caused by the movement of plates. The boundaries of the plates are the weak zones where earthquakes are more likely to occur. The weak zones are also known as seismic or fault zones.

16. (*a*) The Earthquake can cause floods, landslides and tsunamis.

17. (*b*)

18. (*c*) Electrograph is not related to the Earthquake. It is used for tracing actions of electrical devices.

19. (*b*) Tsunamis are caused by earthquake, landslide or volcanic eruptions on the sea floor. An earthquake is caused by the movement of tectonic plates and thus this earthquake on the sea floor can cause tsunamis.

20. (*b*) I. Electroscope is a device which tests whether an object is carrying charge or not.
II. A lightning conductor protects building from the effect of lightning by the process of earthing.
IV. In an electrical storm, the upper portion of the cloud is positive and the lower portion is negative.

21. (*b*)

22. (*c*) If you live in the Earthquake prone area, then
I. You would keep an emergency kit always ready.
II. You would have a closed book shelves and closed cupboards.
III. You would fix the cupboards to the walls.
IV. You would not keep breakable items on the upper shelves.

23. (*c*) For each whole number increase in magnitude, a ten fold increases in the intensity of Earthquake occurs. Thus, the tremors at *B* is 100 times those of place *A*.

Light

1. (*d*) When all the parallel rays reflected from a plane surface are not parallel, the reflection is known as diffused or irregular reflection. For Fig. (*B*), incident rays are parallel but the reflected pattern is not parallel.

2. (*c*) Light can be reflected from any point or part of the mirror.

3. (*b*) When all the parallel rays reflected from a plane surface are not parallel, then reflection is known as diffused or irregular reflection. It is caused by the irregularities in the reflecting surface.

4. (*a*) $\angle AOC + \angle i = 90°$

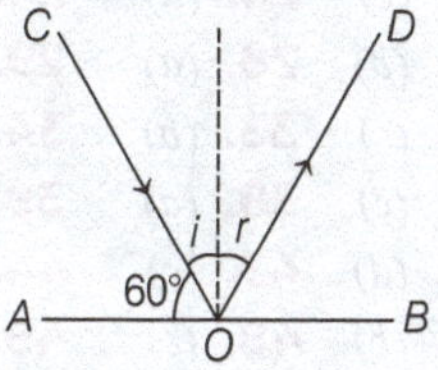

$$\Rightarrow \quad \angle i = 90° - 60° = 30°$$
$$\therefore \quad \angle i = \angle r = 30°$$

5. (*d*) Infinite images are formed when two plane mirrors are placed parallel and facing towards each other with object between them.

6. (*c*) $\angle i + 40° = 90° \Rightarrow \angle i = \angle r = 50°$

7. (*d*) All the rays will follow the laws of reflection. Hence, angle of incidence will always be equal to the angle of reflection in all three cases.

8. (*c*) The image formed by a plane mirror is upright, virtual, of the same size as the object, and as far behind the mirror as the object is in front of it.

9. (*d*) Distance of test card from the plane mirror (behind the mirror) = 150 cm
Distance of man from the mirror = 100 cm
Thus, distance of man from the image of test card = 150 + 100 = 250 cm

10. (*a*) Due to lateral inversion in mirror time 8 : 50 will be seen as 3:10.

11. (*d*) Mirage is an optical illusion which is caused due to atmospheric refraction of light.

12. (*a*) As we move up from ground or surface of Earth, the atmospheric pressure decreases and so, the density of air decreases. This is the cause of optical illusion.

13. (*d*) The ciliary muscles contract and loosen to change the focal length of lens to focus the image of objects at varying distances.

14. (*c*) When we enter in a dark room our pupil expands to allow maximum light to pass through it and it takes some time.

15. (*b*) Rods are the rod-shaped cells of the retina that are sensitive to the dim light.
Cones are cone-shaped cells of the retina that are sensitive to the colours of light.

16. (*b*) Lens in our eyes is convex lens.

17. (*c*) Accommodation is the ability of the eye to change its focus from distant to near objects. It is achieved by changing the shape of eye lens.

18. (*c*) The focal length of the eye lens increases when eye muscles are relaxed and lens becomes thinner. In increasing the focal length the muscles become contracted and lens becomes thicker.

19. (*d*) The iris controls the adjustment of size of pupil for changing brightness of light. It is the coloured part of the eye.

20. (*d*) Rods sense the brightness of light.
Cones functions in bright light and sense the colour of light.

21. (*c*) There is a slight difference between the images formed by left and right eye individually.
Our brain combines both the images to give a three dimensional view.

22. (*c*) The retina of human eye has an ability to retain the image of an object for one-sixteenth of a second even after the removal of the object. This is called persistence of vision and used in moving picture applications like cinematography.

23. (*b*) Sun, stars, glowing tubelight and fire are luminous objects because they emit their own light.
Moon, Earth and table are non-luminous objects because they do not emit their own light.

24. (*a*)

25. (*b*) Diffused reflection is not due to the failure of the laws of reflection. It is caused by the irregularities in the reflecting surface.

26. (*d*)

27. (*b*) A person of 1m long in front of a plane mirror seems to be 1m from the image.
Splitting of white light into its constituent colours is known as dispersion. According to the laws of reflection, $\angle i$ is equal to $\angle r$.

28. (*c*) The correct match of columns is
Cataract → cloudy eye lens
Cornea → front part of eye
Blind spot → junction of optic nerve and retina
Persistence of vision → 1/16th of a second

29. (*a*) The size of the pupil becomes large when you see in dim light. Night birds have less cones then rods in their eyes. Cinematography works on the principle of persistence of vision.

Practice Set 1

1. (*c*)	**2.** (*a*)	**3.** (*d*)	**4.** (*b*)	**5.** (*a*)
6. (*b*)	**7.** (*c*)	**8.** (*b*)	**9.** (*a*)	**10.** (*a*)
11. (*d*)	**12.** (*c*)	**13.** (*b*)	**14.** (*b*)	**15.** (*b*)
16. (*a*)	**17.** (*a*)	**18.** (*a*)	**19.** (*b*)	**20.** (*b*)
21. (*b*)	**22.** (*c*)	**23.** (*a*)	**24.** (*d*)	**25.** (*d*)
26. (*a*)	**27.** (*b*)	**28.** (*a*)	**29.** (*c*)	**30.** (*b*)
31. (*c*)	**32.** (*c*)	**33.** (*b*)	**34.** (*c*)	**35.** (*c*)
36. (*b*)	**37.** (*c*)	**38.** (*a*)	**39.** (*c*)	**40.** (*b*)
41. (*b*)	**42.** (*d*)	**43.** (*c*)	**44.** (*b*)	**45.** (*b*)
46. (*d*)	**47.** (*b*)	**48.** (*c*)	**49.** (*a*)	**50.** (*b*)

Practice Set 2

1. (*c*)	**2.** (*c*)	**3.** (*a*)	**4.** (*b*)	**5.** (*d*)
6. (*a*)	**7.** (*b*)	**8.** (*c*)	**9.** (*a*)	**10.** (*d*)
11. (*b*)	**12.** (*c*)	**13.** (*b*)	**14.** (*c*)	**15.** (*d*)
16. (*c*)	**17.** (*b*)	**18.** (*c*)	**19.** (*c*)	**20.** (*c*)
21. (*a*)	**22.** (*c*)	**23.** (*b*)	**24.** (*b*)	**25.** (*b*)
26. (*a*)	**27.** (*d*)	**28.** (*b*)	**29.** (*b*)	**30.** (*d*)
31. (*a*)	**32.** (*b*)	**33.** (*c*)	**34.** (*d*)	**35.** (*b*)
36. (*c*)	**37.** (*d*)	**38.** (*d*)	**39.** (*d*)	**40.** (*c*)
41. (*c*)	**42.** (*b*)	**43.** (*b*)	**44.** (*c*)	**45.** (*a*)
46. (*a*)	**47.** (*a*)	**48.** (*b*)	**49.** (*c*)	**50.** (*a*)